GW00503749

CHARCUTERIE BOARDS

Table of Contents

Introduction

The charcuterie board is a wonderful delicacy that can be used for breakfast, brunch, snack, lunch or dinner; the recipes contain some suggestions for these selections.

Nowadays, a charcuterie board is often served as an appetizer on restaurant menus, indicating that many people enjoy it. Its farm-to-table concept aligns with today's healthy eating trends, making its natural beauty suitable for a variety of situations - another reason you should try it at your next date.

They are a fantastic conversation starter and meeting area for visitors, in addition to being a great way to exhibit and enjoy the vast assortment of smoked, salted, and cured meats from the world of charcuterie. We now include them in our chef business since they have become so important to our get-togethers. We usually bring a charcuterie board to events and parties to break the ice and open the conversation. When people share their ideas and feelings over food, they feel at ease and connected.

There are several ways to set up a Charcuterie board, and in some situations, specific traditions bind its forms. However, I prefer to assemble my Charcuterie board in the simplest and best way possible by organizing my ingredients around three factors: flavors, tastes, and ease of eating at the table. For me, the objective is to have these three aspects complement each other while remaining true to the Charcuterie board concept.

However, this cookbook focuses on the simple process of arranging party-worthy displays of cured meats, cheeses, fresh and dried fruits, fresh and roasted vegetables, as well as complementing sauces and crackers. We'll teach you how to build perfect charcuterie setups that will have your friends and guests talking throughout this book. There are 120 recipes in all, ranging in size from small to large, for a variety of events.

Our objective for the book is that it will not only guide you through the world of charcuterie and assist you in putting together a beautiful and delectable board, but it will also encourage you to form even deeper bonds with friends and family over a magnificent spread. After all, the art of charcuterie is all about that.

Are you ready to make your delicious Charcuterie Boards? If you're ready to release your creative, adventurous, and fun side, then my Charcuterie Boards are for you.

Chapter 1

Special Boards

10 Mins

0 Mins

6

Fig, Ham, and Spinach Board

 Method

1. To make the dressing, mix the Dijon mustard and lemon juice in a small bowl until smooth. Sprinkle with salt and black pepper after gradually adding olive oil until emulsified.

2. Toss shallots and spinach with dressing in a medium mixing bowl. Spread the spinach mixture over the board, then add the figs, ham, and gorgonzola cheese.

INGREDIENTS

- Dressing:
- 1 tbsp of Dijon mustard
- 1 lemon, juiced
- 1/3 cup of olive oil, extra-virgin
- Salt and black pepper to taste
- Board:
- 2 shallots, thinly sliced
- 2/3 cup of baby spinach
- 12 figs, quartered
- 4 oz of ham
- 1/3 cup of crumbled gorgonzola cheese

Chocolate and Nuts Board

Method

1. Pour about 2 cups of each chocolate sauce into 2 different serving bowls and place them in the center of the board with a 3 to 4-inch gap between them.

2. Arrange the other ingredients in a uniform pattern on the board, around and between the chocolate bowls.

3. Arrange little implements on the board, such as tasting forks, tasting spoons, mini tongs, and so on.

4. The chocolate cutting board can be much more colorful if it is the right season for strawberries. Set a bowl with melted chocolate, and a bowl with strawberries, and place 5 strawberries with chocolate-covered tips on top of the cutting board

10 Mins

0 Mins

6

INGREDIENTS

- Dark chocolate sauce
- Milk chocolate sauce
- 1 cup of sweet or semi-sweet chocolate
- 2/3 cup of assorted toasted nuts
- 1 cup of mixed fresh berries (strawberries, raspberries) 2 large bananas, peeled and sliced
- ½ cup of cubed pound cake
- ½ cup of chocolate cookies (like Oreos) Mini muffins Mini croissants

10 Mins

0 Mins

6

VIP Cheese Board

 Method

1. Set aside separate serving dishes with cherry preserves, raspberry jam, honey, and butter.
2. Put the remaining ingredients on a big board in the same manner.
3. To serve, spread cherry preserves, raspberry jam, honey, and butter on the sides.

INGREDIENTS

- Cherry preserves
- Raspberry jam
- Honey
- Butter
- 8 oz of cured meats, thinly sliced
- 2 baguettes, sliced diagonally, ½-inch thick
- 4 oz of blue cheese
- 4 oz of sharp cheddar, thickly sliced
- 4 oz of Gruyere cheese, thickly sliced
- 4 red apples, cored and sliced
- 4 pears, cored and halved or sliced
- 2 oz of dried figs, quartered
- Toasted cashews
- Water crackers

Summer Blossom Board

INGREDIENTS

- Mini baguettes, sliced diagonally, ½-inch thick
- Extra-virgin olive oil for brushing
- ½ tsp of garlic powder
- ½ tsp of spicy paprika
- Salt to taste
- Mixed cured meats
- Swiss cheese, thickly sliced
- Manchego cheese, thickly sliced
- ½ cup of semi-dried tomatoes
- 1 lb. of green grapes
- 2 cups of dried apricot
- Water crackers
- Chips
- 1 cup of caponata
- 1 cup of green olives, pitted
- 1 cup of toasted walnuts or your favorite nuts

10 Mins

5 Mins

6

Method

1. Preheat the oven to 400 °F and line a baking sheet with baguette pieces. llive oil should be brushed over the surface. After that, sprinkle with garlic powder, paprika, and salt. Toast the bread for 5 minutes in the oven, or until golden brown.
2. In the meantime, spread the remaining items on a big board, including cured meats, cheeses, tomatoes, grapes, apricots, water crackers, and chips.
3. Place caponata, olives, and walnuts in separate small dishes. Place the bowls on the boards.
4. Serve with baguette slices.

Spanish Classic Board

10 Mins

0 Mins

6

 Method

1. Combine caponata, bruschetta, caper berries, olives, and artichoke halves in separate serving dishes. Arrange the bowls on the board.
2. Place the remaining ingredients on a serving board, top with edible flowers, and serve with cutlery.

INGREDIENTS

- 1 cup of eggplant caponata
- 1 cup of roasted pepper bruschetta
- 1 cup of aper berries
- 1 cup olives of choice
- 1 cup of grilled artichoke halves Toasted crostini slices
- 4 types of your favorite cheese
- Assorted dried fruits (mangoes, apricots, tomatoes, pineapples, etc.)
- Assorted fresh fruits (berries, clementine sections, grapes, etc.)
- Assorted crackers, chips, and breadsticks
- Mixed cured meats of choice (salami, prosciutto, dried beef, etc.)
- Edible flowers to garnish

INGREDIENTS

- 1 cup of marinated artichoke hearts, drained
- 1 cup of mixed pitted olives, drained
- ½ cup of peppadew peppers
- ½ cup of Marcona almonds
- 8 oz of mozzarella balls
- 1 tbsp of olive oil
- A pinch red chili flakes
- 1 tbsp of chopped fresh parsley
- 8 oz of Asiago cheese, thinly sliced
- 8 oz of provolone cheese, thinly sliced
- 8 oz of Parmesan cheese, cubed
- Assorted cured meats, thinly sliced
- 1 loaf of focaccia bread, toasted and sliced

Antipasto Starter

Board

 Method

1. Place cherry preserves, raspberry jam, honey, and butter on separate serving plates.
2. Repeat with the remaining ingredients on a large board.
3. To serve, spread the sides of the plate with cherry preserves, raspberry jam, honey, and butter.

10 Mins

0 Mins

6

10 Mins

0 Mins

6

Straightforward Charcuterie Board

Method

1. Arrange the preserves of berry in a serving dish on the board. Serve with the remaining ingredients on the board.

INGREDIENTS

- 1 cup of berry preserves
- 1 cup of salami slices
- 1 cup of prosciutto slices
- 1 cup of toasted pecans
- 3 cheese types of choice

INGREDIENTS

- ¼ cup of tapenade
- 3 lightly toasted flatbreads, cut into halves
- 6 oz of thinly sliced cured meat of choice
- 4 oz of burrata
- 2 tbsp of crushed toasted almonds
- Red chili flakes for topping
- Honey for drizzling

Easy Charcuterie Flatbreads Board

 Method

1. Place half of the tapenade on one side of each flatbread and place it on the board.
2. Arrange the cured meat, half of the burrata, almonds, red chili flakes, and honey on top. Serve with the rest of the tapenade and the burrata.

10 Mins

0 Mins

6

INGREDIENTS

- ¾ cup of ricotta cheese
- ¾ cup of prune jam
- ½ cup of pimiento-stuffed green olives
- ½ cup of roasted almonds
- 6 oz of Manchego cheese, thickly sliced 9 oz of prosciutto, rolled 1 cup of chocolate pretzels
- 1 ½ cups of assorted crackers
- 6 oz of dried prunes
- 6 oz of salted dark chocolate bars, broken into pieces
- 8 ounces of caramel truffles
- Butterscotch sweets

Fall Charcuterie Board 1

 Method

1. Combine ricotta cheese, prune jam, and olives in separate dishes. Place bowls on the board and evenly divide the remaining ingredients. After that, serve.

10 Mins

0 Mins

6

Loaded Brunch Board

10 Mins

0 Mins

6

Method

1. Combine the fruit jam(s), maple syrup, Greek yogurt, and chocolate spread dip in separate dishes. Place on various parts of the board.
2. Place poached eggs or cooked egg slices in the center of the board.
3. Put the remaining ingredients in a similar pattern all over the board and serve.

INGREDIENTS

- Fruit jam (s)
- Honey or maple syrup
- Greek yogurt
- Chocolate spread dip
- 6 poached eggs
- Pancakes, pre-made
- Waffles, pre-made
- Donuts, pre-made
- 1 ½ cups of cheddar cheese cubes
- 1 cup of Gruyere cheese cubes
- Cured meats (salami, sausages, prosciutto, cooked bacon, smoked salmon, etc.)
- Fresh fruits (mixed berries, pineapples, watermelon, grapes, sweet orange sections, sliced apples, sliced pears, etc.)
- 1 ½ cups of mixed nuts (pecans, walnuts, macadamia nuts, almonds, pistachios, etc.)

INGREDIENTS

- Fig spread
- Honey
- 7 oz of cheddar cheese wedge
- 7 oz of Mimolette wedge
- 4 oz of log goat cheese
- Assorted cured meats
- 1 cup of toasted cashew nuts
- 1 cup of toasted pecans
- ½ cup of pitted mixed olives
- Fresh fruits (sectioned clementines, grapes, sliced pears)
- ½ cup of dried apricots
- Flatbread slices, crackers, and chips

Southern Style
Charcuterie Board

 Method

1. Mix the fig spread and honey in separate dishes. Place bowls in the center of the board and evenly distribute the remaining ingredients around it. Serve!

10 Mins

0 Mins

6

INGREDIENTS

- 1 cup of artichoke spread
- 1 cup of roasted red pepper spread
- Honey
- 9 oz of blue cheese wedge
- 9 oz of goat cheese wedge Cured meats
- Mixed toasted nuts
- 1 cup of dried figs, halved
- 1 cup of dried cherries
- ½ cup of pomegranate seeds
- Fresh berries
- Pitted black olives
- Caperberries
- 2 small Fuyu persimmons
- 1 rosemary sprig to garnish
- 1 sourdough bread, sliced
- Crackers and chips

Fall Charcuterie

Board 2

Method

1. Combine artichoke spread, red pepper spread, and honey in separate dishes. Place dishes on opposite ends of the board and evenly distribute the remaining ingredients across the board. Serve!

10 Mins

0 Mins

6

INGREDIENTS

- Water crackers
- 1 baguette, sliced and toasted
- 9 oz of wedge cranberry cheese
- 1 cup of goat cheese
- Triple cream soft ripened cheese
- Cured meats (chorizo, chili salami, Sopressata, prosciutto, ham)
- Fruits (red grapes and pickled cranberries)
- Whole grain mustard, in serving bowl
- Tapenade, in serving bowl
- Berry jam, in serving bowl

Winter Cuddle Board

 Method

1. Arrange all ingredients on board and enjoy!

10 Mins

0 Mins

6

10 Mins

0 Mins

6

Keto Charcuterie

Board

Method

1. Arrange all ingredients across board and enjoy immediately.

INGREDIENTS

- Cheeses (Smoked gouda, cheddar, blue cheese, goat cheese, brie cheese)
- Cured protein (smoked salmon, prosciutto, salami, pepperoni, grilled shrimp, beef jerky)
- Fruits (mixed berries, avocado slices, mixed olives)
- Nuts (almonds, pecans, macadamia nuts, pili nuts)
- Vegetables (cucumber slices, cherry tomato halves, sliced zucchinis, sliced red bell peppers, steamed cauliflower florets)
- Dips (ranch dip, cheese dip), in serving bowls
- Snacks (pork rinds, keto crackers, parsnip chips, cheese crisps)

INGREDIENTS

- Snacks (apple chips, muddy buddies, dragon fruit chips, crackers, longan puffs, pretzels)
- Fruits (strawberries, raspberries, red grapes, apple slices, sugared cranberries, dried dates)
- Sweets (mini marshmallows, mini peanut butter cups, white and dark chocolate cubes)
- Nuts (pistachios, pecans, macadamia nuts)
- Chocolate sauce, in serving bowl
- Fruit dip, in serving bowl
- Caramel sauce, in serving bowl

Happy Dessert Board

Method

1. Arrange all ingredients on board identically and enjoy!

10 Mins

0 Mins

6

Dinner

Charcuterie Board

10 Mins

0 Mins

6

 Method

Arrange all ingredients on board identically and enjoy!

INGREDIENTS

- Assorted cured meats (cooked bacon, assorted salami, prosciutto, beef jerky)
- Mixed vegetables (roasted cauliflower florets, whole roasted tomatoes, roasted bell peppers, cucumber slices, sliced radishes, etc.)
- Cheeses (cheddar, mozzarella balls. Parmesan cheese, ricotta, smoked Gouda)
- Fruits (dried fig quarters, blackberries, dried apricots, apples, pears, grapes, olives)
- Sauces (hummus, tapenade, white bean dip, ricotta spread, smoked tuna dip, pesto)
- Salads (tuna salad,
- Caprese salad, or your choice of salad)

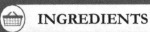

- Mixed fresh fruits (strawberries, raspberries, blueberries, and red grapes)
- Water crackers, chips, and chocolate biscuits
- Salami slices
- Cherry tomatoes
- Cheeses (Gruyere slices, white cheddar slices)
- Red jelly sweets
- Blue jelly sweets

Patriotic Charcuterie Board

 Method

1. Arrange blueberries in a small dish in the center of the board.
2. Spread the rest of the ingredients evenly around the board. Enjoy!

10 Mins

0 Mins

6

10 Mins

0 Mins

6

Gluten-Free Charcuterie Board

 **Method**

1. Arrange all ingredients on board identically and enjoy!

INGREDIENTS

- Cured meats (cooked bacon, salami, prosciutto, capicola_
- Cheeses (hard goat cheese, baked brie, soft goat cheese pecorino romano)
- Nuts (pecans, pistachios, walnuts, hazelnuts)
- Butter and dips (cashew butter, strawberry dip, cherry dip, pumpkin butter), in serving bowls
- Fresh fruits (pomegranate, berries, sweet orange sections, apples, pears, pitted olives, grapes)
- Dried fruits (apricots, figs, dates, cranberries)
- Glute-free crackers
- Pickles
- Roasted veggies (asparagus, broccoli, potatoes)

10 Mins

0 Mins

6

Simple Lunch

Charcuterie Board

Method

1. Arrange all ingredients on board identically and enjoy!

INGREDIENTS

- 1 large carrot, peeled and julienned
- 1 large red bell pepper, deseeded and julienned
- 1 cup of cherry tomatoes, halved
- 1 cup of fresh blueberries
- Dips (hummus, salmon pate, cottage cheese), in serving bowls)
- ½ cup of toasted walnuts
- 6 hard-boiled eggs, halved
- Cheese slices (cheddar, Gruyere, and manchego)
- Cured meats (salami, prosciutto)
- Pita bread wedges
- Crackers

10 Mins

0 Mins

6

Barbecue Charcuterie Board

Method

1. Identically, group all ingredients on board and enjoy!

INGREDIENTS

- 1 lb. of grilled beef brisket, thinly sliced
- 1 lb. of grilled chicken thighs, shredded
- 3 cups of barbecue sauce, of your choice
- 4 oz each of cheese slices (white cheddar, pepper Jack, Colby Jack)
- ½ cup each of dried fruits (cherries, apricots)
- ½ cup of sliced pimento peppers
- ½ cup of baby pickles
- ¼ cup of fruit jam of your choice, in serving bowl
- ¼ cup of mustard, in serving bowl
- Assorted crackers
- ¼ cup of fruit jam of your choice, in serving bowl
- ¼ cup of mustard, in serving bowl
- Assorted crackers

10 Mins

0 Mins

1

Mini Individual
Charcuterie Board

 Method

1. On a small board, arrange all of the ingredients and serve with hummus and jam.

 INGREDIENTS

- ½ cup of cheddar cheese cubes
- 4 slices of blue cheese
- 4 slices of white cheddar cheese
- 3 slices of soft goat cheese
- Cured meats (prosciutto, salami)
- Crackers
- Fruit jam, in serving bowl
- Hummus, in serving bowl

INGREDIENTS

- 3 large baguettes, cut into ½-inch thick slices
- 1 medium red onion, thinly sliced
- ½ cup of dill pickles, thinly sliced
- Italian dried salami, folded in halves
- Black forest ham slices, rolled
- Roasted turkey breasts, thinly sliced
- 1 cup of cherry tomatoes, halved
- 1 cup of sliced Parmesan cheese
- 1 cup of sliced white cheddar cheese
- Mayonnaise, in serving bowl
- Mustard, in serving bowl
- Hot sauce, in serving bowl

Deli Sandwich Board

 Method

1. In round board, arrange baguette slices around.
2. Group remaining ingredients in center of baguette layout. Enjoy!

10 Mins

0 Mins

6

10 Mins

0 Mins

6

Plant-Based Charcuterie Board

Method

1. Arrange all ingredients on board identically and enjoy!

INGREDIENTS

- 1 ½ cups of celery sticks, cut into thirds
- 1 ½ cups of radish slices
- Dips (almond dip, cashew chip), in serving bowls
- Toasted nuts (almonds, cashews, pecans)
- Toasted seeds (sunflower seeds, pumpkin seeds, sesame seeds)
- Fruits (grapes, lemon wedges, pitted Kalamata olives)
- Plant-based crackers
- Cheeses (vegan feta cheese, vegan cheddar cheese)
- Teriyaki tofu cubes

10 Mins

0 Mins

6

Cheese and Meat

Board

Method

1. Each ingredient should be grouped, layered, and arranged in piles.

INGREDIENTS

- Boursin Cheese
- Stilton Cheese
- Brie
- salumi
- prosciutto
- olives
- sliced pears
- dried apricots
- raspberries
- dried nuts
- honey
- variety of crackers

10 Mins

0 Mins

6

Easy Fall Apple and

Cheese Board

Method

1. Arrange your cheeses on a chopping board. If desired, slice one of the cheeses ahead of time.
2. Arrange the condiments (caramel sauce, honey, and mustard) on the board in small serving dishes.
3. Surround the cheeses with crackers and pretzels.
4. Toss in a couple of whole apples as well as a bunch of apple pieces.
5. Use dried apples and caramel candies to fill in the spaces.
6. Finish with a leaf garnish.

INGREDIENTS

- Smoked Gouda, Jarlsberg (similar to Swiss), and Peppercorn
- Cheddar
- honey
- The Best Caramel Dip (1 cup)
- whole grain
- mustard
- red and green apples, whole and sliced
- caramel candies
- dried apples
- assorted crackers
- mini pretzels
- apple and/or fall leaves for garnish
- board
- cheese knives

15 Mins

0 Mins

6

Winter Cheese Board

Method

1. Distribute honeycomb and cheeses around the board's corners, fanning cheese slices slightly.
2. Use clementines, olives, and walnuts to fill in wide spaces, then cornichons, figs, and rosemary sprigs to fill in smaller spaces.
3. Serve with crackers or pita chips and, of course, red wine.

INGREDIENTS

- 1 square of honeycomb
- 4 ounces of sliced merlot Bellavitano (Sartori)
- 4 ounces of sliced rosemary Asiago
- 4 ounces of Gorgonzola
- 2 ounces of sliced aged Parmesan
- 2 clementines, peeled and segmented
- ½ cup of Castelvetrano olives
- ½ cup of toasted walnuts
- ½ cup of cornichons
- 4 dried figs, halved
- Rosemary sprigs, for garnish (optional)
- Crackers or homemade pita chips
- Red wine of choice

10 Mins

0 Mins

6

Fruit and Chocolate Dessert Board

Method

1. Arrange all ingredients on board and enjoy!

INGREDIENTS

Chocolate:
- Dark Chocolate Cherry Almond Bark
- Dark Chocolate Pineapple Almond Ginger Bark
- White Chocolate Cranberry Pistachio Bark
- Orange-Peach Dark Chocolate Bites
- Dark Chocolate Almond Blueberry Swiss Bar

Cheese:
- French Brie
- Cranberry Goat Cheese "heart"
- Wine Rubbed Italian Blue Cheese with wine-soaked Cranberries
- Vermont Artisan Cheese

Fruit:
- Pomegranate
- Grapes
- Blackberries
- Strawberries
- Pears
- Accompaniments:
- Chocolate Cookie Crisps
- Chocolate Chip Cookie
- Crisps
- Biscotti
- Cinnamon Raisin Bread
- Simple water crackers
- Hear-shaped donuts (for
- Valentine's day) Sugared Pecans
- Almonds

15 Mins

10 Mins

6

Grilled Fruit Cheese Board

Method

1. Drizzle the fruit with olive oil after slicing it.
2. Place fruit on a grill pan and cook over medium-high heat until tender but not mushy. Set aside and allow it to cool.
3. Arrange grilled fruit pieces, cheeses, and crackers on the board in a circular pattern.
4. Add herbs and flowers.

INGREDIENTS

- 3 tablespoons of olive oil
- Peach, sliced
- Avocado, sliced
- Pear, sliced
- Pineapple, sliced
- Membrillo, quince paste
- Water crackers or crackers or your choice
- Flour tortillas, cut into wedges
- Honey
- Jam or preserves of your choice
- Assorted soft and hard cheeses
- Fresh herbs: mint and basil

INGREDIENTS

- Various cheese (get a mix of flavors, textures, shapes, and colors)
- Salty items (meats, nuts, olives, etc.)
- Sweet items (fruit, dried fruit, chocolate, etc.)
- Crunchy items (crackers, pita chips, breadsticks, etc.)
- Condiments (honey, mustards, chutney, etc.)
- Space-filling items (grapes, cherry tomatoes, cherries)
- Garnish (fresh herbs)
- Cheese board (can use a cheese board, cutting board, serving platter, tray, or cookie sheet)
- Cheese knives

Bruschetta Bar

Method

1. Start by evenly distributing the cheese wedges, logs, and wheels around the cheese board surface. Add cheese knives to the mix.
2. Place the salty ingredients around the cheese.
3. Finally, add a couple of piles of sweet ingredients.
4. Fill small jars or bowls with crunchy foods and sauces.
5. Use space-filling ingredients like grapes, cherry tomatoes, or cherries to fill in any empty spots.
6. Finally, add fresh herbs to the cheeseboard.

10 Mins

0 Mins

6

- 1 Dragon's Breath Blue Cheese Ball, cut in half
- nuts
- figs, sliced in half
- pears, sliced
- raspberries
- blackberries
- little dish of honey
- savour jams, like pear and roasted garlic
- mini pastries
- nougat, cut into bite sized chunks
- chocolate
- oat crackers (or you favourite crackers)

Dessert Cheese Plate

 Method

1. Cut the Dragon's Breath Blue cheese in half and serve using a small cheese knife.
2. Place the halves in the cheese plate's center.
3. Surround the cheese with the remaining ingredients.

20 Mins

0 Mins

6

Chapter 2

Small Boards

0 Mins

0 Mins

2

PICNIC IN PARIS

INGREDIENTS

- 4 ounces of saucisson sec, thinly sliced
- 2 pears
- 7 ounces of double-cream brie
- 2 tablespoons of whole-grain mustard
- 3 ounces of pâté
- 1 baguette

Method

1. Prepare the ingredients once you get to your destination by thinly slicing the saucisson sec and placing it on a corner of the cutting board.
2. Peel and slice the pears, then arrange them in the opposite corner.
3. Add the brie towards the c enter but shifted to one of the corners.
4. Next to the brie, add a teaspoon of mustard.
5. Put a tiny spoonful of pâté into the pear slices.
6. Tear the baguette in half and stack it on the board or next to it.

Serving Suggestions: A great combination to compliment the richness of the pâté and brie is La Mauriane, a French red wine perfumed with black plum, blackberries, and wildflowers.

10 Mins

7 Mins

2

EUROPEAN BREAKFAST IN BED

INGREDIENTS

- 3 croissants
- 4 ounces of gruyère (or Swiss cheese), thinly sliced
- 3 ounces of prosciutto, thinly sliced
- ¼ cup of citrus marmalade
- 1 tablespoon confectioners' sugar

Method

1. Preheat the oven to 375°F.
2. Toast the croissants for 5 to 7 mins on a rimmed baking sheet.
3. In the meantime, finely slice the gruyère and place the pieces on one of the platter's corners.
4. Split the prosciutto pieces and arrange them on the tray close to each other.
5. Using a small spoon, scrape the marmalade into a small bowl. Place it on the dish with a napkin beneath it to prevent it from sliding.
6. Take the croissants out of the oven and arrange them in the center of the tray. Dust one with confectioners' sugar using a small fine-mesh sieve. The other two may be left alone.

Serving Suggestions: You can never make the wrong decision with freshly squeezed orange juice. Serve some sparkling Italian prosecco if you're in the mood for a mimosa.

0 Mins

0 Mins

2

JAMÓN EXPERIENCE

 **Method**

1. Fill a small bowl with Castelvetrano olives and put it at the board's upper right corner.

2. Fold the jamón gently into wavy ribbons towards the board's center top.

3. Arrange the Manchego pieces below the jamón in the center of the board, roughly broken.

4. Cut the baguette in half using a knife. Leave one-half intact and slice the other half open with a sharp knife.

5. Brush a tiny bit of olive oil inside the cut baguette pieces, then season with sea salt on the oiled sides. Apply a single coat of oil to the top of the uncut piece. Place the bread on the board's left side.

Serving Suggestions: Manzanilla is a chilled Spanish sherry that goes well with cured meats and seafood. It has a dry, crisp, and light floral palate with chamomile, almonds, and yeast flavors. It pairs nicely with jamón and this tapas-style buffet.

INGREDIENTS

- 1 cup of Castelvetrano olives (or any mild green olive), not pitted
- 6 ounces of jamón ibérico (or prosciutto), thinly sliced
- 4 ounces of Manchego (or any mild sheep milk cheese), broken into rough pieces
- 1 baguette
- 2 tablespoons of garlic-infused olive oil
- Sea salt

0 Mins

0 Mins

2

KIDS IN BOLOGNA

INGREDIENTS

- 6 grissini sticks
- Small bundle fresh basil leaves
- 2 tablespoons of balsamic reduction or glaze
- 1 cup of cherry tomatoes
- 8 ounces of fresh mozzarella bocconcini (or fresh mozzarella cut into bite-size pieces)
- 4 ounces of mortadella (or any mild deli meat), thinly sliced

Method

1. Put the grissini in a glass that is slightly offset from the middle of the board and sticks straight up.

2. Arrange the basil bundle and a little dish of balsamic reduction at the bottom of the grissini glass.

3. Split the board into thirds visually (picture a peace symbol) and arrange the cherry tomatoes, bocconcini, and mortadella in separate sections.

Serving Suggestions: For each serving, blend a half cup of whole milk and a quarter cup of chocolate syrup together.

45 Mins

0 Mins

2

SALAMI KETO LOVERS

 INGREDIENTS

- 1 cup of fresh garlic ricotta
- 4 Mini Chaffles
- Extra-virgin olive oil, for drizzling
- Freshly ground black pepper
- 3 ounces of salami picante, casing removed, thinly sliced
- 3 ounces of Creminelli Whiskey Salami Minis (or any mild salami)

 **Method**

1. Follow the instructions for making the fresh garlic ricotta and chaffles. The ricotta may be made ahead of time and kept refrigerated for up to a week, but the chaffles are best served at room temperature.

2. Using a spoon, put the ricotta into a small bowl towards the middle of the board, but slightly to the left. Spray it with olive oil and season it with pepper.

3. Place the chaffles to the right of the ricotta, stacking them to make a nice presentation.

4. Layer the salami pieces on top of the ricotta.

5. Place the mini salami sticks at the top left corner of the board in a small upright dish or glass.

Serving Suggestions: Mix 3 cups filtered water, ¼ teaspoon sea salt, 130 mg potassium powder, and 45 mg magnesium powder in a pitcher. Squeeze in half a lemon juice and whisk well to blend.

 3 hrs

 0 Mins

 2

SUMMER BERRY FIELDS

 Method

1. Heat the oil in a large skillet over high heat. Spray with olive oil and add the pancetta. Heat for 6 to 8 minutes, or until the pancetta crisps up like cooked bacon.

2. Combine the granulated sugar and lemon juice in a medium mixing dish. Gently toss in the blackberries and raspberries to coat them in the mixture. Set aside for 5 minutes to steep.

3. Spread the butter on the brioche pieces and toast them. From the top to just below the center, place the brioche down the left side of the board. Place Macerated raspberries and blackberries on top of the brioche. Finish with a cinnamon and confectioners' sugar sprinkle.

4. Place the mascarpone in a heap in the brioche's lower right corner

5. Place the crispy pancetta on the top right corner of the board

6. Pile the oven-dried strawberries in a small bowl, and place it in the bottom left corner with a small serving spoon next to it.

7. Place the honey in a small jar with a honey wand Just above or next to the strawberries, .

 INGREDIENTS

- 1 cup of fresh garlic ricotta
- 1 cup of Oven-Dried Strawberries
- 4 ounces of pancetta, thinly sliced
- 1 tablespoon of olive oil
- 1 tablespoon of granulated sugar
- 2 teaspoons of lemon juice
- ½ cup of blackberries
- 1 cup of raspberries
- 4 thick slices of brioche
- 2 tablespoons of unsalted butter
- Pinch ground cinnamon
- Pinch confectioners' sugar
- 8 ounces of mascarpone cheese
- 2 tablespoons of honey

Serving Suggestions: This board goes well with a glass of French champagne. If you're celebrating and want to go all out, Dom Pérignon is the way to go, but if you want something more modest but still elegant, fresh, and light, a true Brut like Canard-Duchêne is a perfect option.

45 Mins

0 Mins

2

CHERRIES AND ALMONDS

 INGREDIENTS

- ½ cup of Pecan Granola
- 2 cups of plain Greek yogurt
- 4 ounces of bresaola (or lonzino), thinly sliced
- 2 cups of cherries
- 1 cup of Marcona almonds (or any salted blanched almonds)
- 5 to 6 ounces of honeycomb squares

 Method

1. Make the pecan granola according to the directions. You may make the granola up to a month ahead of schedule.

2. Split the Greek yogurt into two small dishes and sprinkle half of the pecan granola on top of each. With a spoon in each dish, arrange the bowls beside each other in the center of a big board.

3. Place the bresaola in the upper right corner.

4. Place the cherries in the bottom left corner.

5. Arrange the Marcona almonds on top of the cherries.

6. Using a tiny knife, put the honeycomb squares to the bottom right.

Serving Suggestions: This board's richness and textures make for a fascinating match with kriek, a hoppy, cherry-flavored Belgian beer produced with sour cherries. Strange Craft Beer Company makes an excellent one, but Lindemans Brewery's kriek lambic beer in Belgium is the real deal.

50 Mins

0 Mins

2

AFTERNOON FOR TWO

INGREDIENTS

- ¼ cup of Pancetta-Onion Jam
- 2 tablespoons of Cabernet Balsamic Reduction
- 8 ounces of burrata (or fresh mozzarella)
- 1 cup of arugula
- Sea salt
- Freshly ground black pepper
- Extra-virgin olive oil
- 4 ounces of Barolo salami (or any richly seasoned salami), thinly sliced
- 2 small loaves of fougasse (or focaccia or ciabatta)

 Method

1. Follow the directions for the pancetta-onion jam and cabernet balsamic reduction. The jam can be made up to two weeks in advance, and the reduction up to three months.

2. Arrange the burrata in the center of a small board and top with arugula, allowing the arugula to cascade around the cheese. Salt, pepper, and a sprinkle of olive oil to taste. Put the burrata next to the cheese knife.

3. Place the pancetta jam towards the base of the burrata in the bottom left corner.

4. In a small bowl, pour the cabernet balsamic reduction and set it in the right upper corner with a little spoon.

5. Place the salami in the right corner, near the balsamic reduction.

6. Tear the bread into little pieces and sprinkle them across the bottom right corner.

Serving Suggestions: The rich aromas of the Barolo salami, pancetta-onion jam, and balsamic reduction are beautifully complemented by Cabernet Sauvignon, a delicious and fruity full-bodied red wine. You can't go wrong if you just pick your favorite bottle.

Chapter 3

Medium Boards

THE SICILIAN TABLE

 **INGREDIENTS**

- 2 cups of Rosemary-Lemon Castelvetrano Olives
- 1 Artisan Focaccia, cut into large squares
- 1 (4-ounce) log goat cheese
- ¼ cup of chopped salted pistachios
- 5½ ounces of salami with pistachios (or any flavorful salami), sliced
- 5½ ounces of fennel salami (or any herb-infused salami), sliced

Method

1. Follow the instructions for preparing the rosemary-lemon olives and artisan focaccia. The olives may be made ahead of time for up to a week, but the focaccia is best served warm or at room temperature.
2. Wrap the goat cheese log in pistachios that have been chopped. Place the log on the board's left-center. Insert a little cheese knife through the top.
3. Arrange the pistachio salami slices in the board's left bottom corner.
4. Place the fennel salami on the board's bottom right corner.
5. Place the marinated olives in a medium bowl with a spoon in the upper right corner of the board.
6. Arrange the focaccia squares over the top of the board, alternating sides.

Serving Suggestions: This board may be paired with an olive vermouth to keep with the concept.

70 Mins

0 Mins

4

SOUTH OF FRANCE

 INGREDIENTS

- 12 ounces of Duck Confit
- ½ cup of Mustard Gastrique
- 8 ounces of fromage blanc (or quark)
- 2 ounces of caviar
- 4 large hard-boiled eggs, diced small
- 1 small red onion, minced
- 6 ounces of black pepper crackers

 Method

1. Follow the instructions for the duck confit and mustard gastrique.
2. Using a serving fork, put the heated duck confit into a small dish and set it on the top left side of the board.
3. On the bottom right side of the board, place the fromage blanc in a small dish with a spoon.
4. In the middle of the board, place the caviar in a small dish with the caviar spoon. Set the teaspoons next to it.
5. Place the diced hard-boiled eggs to the left of the caviar. Place the minced red onion just over the eggs.
6. Spoon the heated mustard gastrique straight onto the board below the caviar, then drag it to the right with the back of the spoon to create an elegant effect. Remove the spoon and set it to the side.
7. Place the crackers in the upper right and lower left quadrants, respectively.

2hrs 25 Mins

0 Mins

4

Serving Suggestions: I suggest Le Mesnil Blanc de Blancs Grand Cru, which offers a delicate fruitiness with touches of apple and pear.

SWEET BELGIUM

INGREDIENTS

- 1 cup of Date Caramel
- 5½ ounces of chocolate salami (or dark chocolate)
- 5 ounces of fromage de Bruxelles (or any soft cow milk cheese, or double-cream brie)
- 4 hazelnut croissants (or plain croissants spread with Nutella)
- 4 plain croissants
- 1 cup of raspberries
- 2 cups of strawberries

Method

1. Follow the directions to make the date caramel spread. This may be made up to 3 days ahead of time if required, but it's best served right away.
2. Make thin rounds out of half of the chocolate salami. Place the slices at the bottom right corner of the board, together with the remaining large piece. Next to it, place a small knife.
3. Using a cheese knife, arrange the fromage de Bruxelles in the center of the board.
4. Set the date caramel spread in a small dish with a spoon in the top right corner of the board and place the bowl in the top right corner of the board.
5. Arrange the croissants on the board's left side.
6. Arrange the raspberries on one side of the fromage, cascading down the other.
7. Use the strawberries to fill in the spaces around the date caramel dish.

Serving Suggestions: To drink with this board, an espresso martini is highly recommended.

10 Mins

0 Mins

4

HUNTING IN MANCHESTER

INGREDIENTS

- 1 cup of Caramelized Onion Dip
- 8 Yorkshire Puddings
- 5½ ounces of wild boar salami (or any bold-flavored salami)
- 1 bundle of chives, finely chopped
- 6 ounces of drunken goat cheese (or sweet goat cheese)
- 6½ ounces of duck jerky (or turkey jerky), cut into thin pieces

Method

1. Prepare the caramelized onion dip and Yorkshire puddings according to the directions.
2. Remove the casing from the wild boar salami and thinly slice about half of it. Place the slices and the remaining big piece in the bottom left quadrant of the board with a small knife.
3. In the upper left corner, place the onion dip dish, chives on top, and a small spoon next to it.
4. Place all of the Yorkshire puddings around the dish to the right of the onion dip.
5. In the lower right corner of the board, approximately 2 inches from one end, softly crumble the goat cheese. Then, using a cheese knife, chop the remaining cheese.
6. Place the jerky pieces next to the cheese in an open area.

1 hr 15 Mins

0 Mins

4

Serving Suggestions: I suggest pairing this board with High West Campfire Whiskey

ROMAN WINTER

INGREDIENTS

- 1 cup of Cabernet Balsamic Reduction
- 1 Artisan Focaccia
- 6 ounces of pastrami, thinly sliced
- 6 ounces of prosciutto cotto (or country ham), thinly sliced
- 8 ounces of fresh mozzarella
- 8 ounces of pecorino romano (or Parmesan)
- 1 bunch of fresh basil
- Extra-virgin olive oil, for drizzling

Method

1. Follow the instructions for preparing the cabernet balsamic reduction and focaccia.
2. Separate the pastrami and prosciutto cotto in the center of the board.
3. In the top right corner, place the fresh mozzarella, and in the bottom left corner, place the pecorino romano wedge. Place one pronged cheese knife near the mozzarella and the other near the pecorino.
4. Place the basil bundle next to the mozzarella.
5. Place the jar of balsamic reduction next to the mozzarella in the upper right corner.
6. Tear or cut the focaccia into large bits and arrange them in the top left corner.
7. Place an olive oil bottle near the board for sprinkling.

Serving Suggestions: I suggest pairing this board with Birra Moretti . Serve it chilled in frosty glasses.

1hr 20 Mins

0 Mins

4

HIGH TEA

INGREDIENTS

- 12 pieces of Thyme Shortbread
- ½ cup of cream cheese
- 8 slices of white bread
- 1 English cucumber, thinly sliced
- 5½ ounces of cranberry Wensleydale cheese (or fruit-infused stilton)
- 7 ounces of Cheshire cheese (or mild cheddar)
- 4 ounces of country ham, thinly sliced
- 1 bunch of green grapes

Method

1. Make the thyme shortbread according to the given directions. You may make the shortbread up to a week beforehand.
2. Spread cream cheese equally on 4 pieces of bread to make cucumber sandwiches. Thin cucumber slices should be strewn over the cream cheese. Another slice of bread should be placed on top of each sandwich. Remove the crusts from each sandwich, then cut each diagonally into quarters and put aside.
3. Arrange the cranberry Wensleydale in the platter's upper left corner. Leave a cheese knife hanging out of the top and crumble a few pieces off one corner.
4. Place the Cheshire in the bottom right corner with a cheese knife.
5. Arrange the ham slices in a loose pattern directly above the Cheshire, filling the top right corner.
6. Place the thyme shortbread cookies in the board's bottom left corner.
7. In the center of the board, dump a heaping quantity of green grapes, allowing the bunches to touch the edges of the cheeses and ham.
8. Place the cucumber sandwiches in the middle left corner of the board, stacked and arranged.

   Serving Suggestions: A selection of herbal and green teas will provide a lighter source of refreshment. Some of my favorites include cranberry hibiscus, rooibos, chamomile, and peppermint green tea.

40 Mins

0 Mins

4

EVERYTHING BRUNCH

INGREDIENTS

- 1 Everything Lavash
- 12 ounces of smoked salmon, sliced
- 1 cup of cream cheese
- 1 bunch of fresh dill, torn into small pieces
- 1 bunch of fresh chives, minced
- 6 vine-ripened Campari tomatoes (or grape tomatoes)
- 1 (3.5-ounce) jar capers, drained
- 1 red onion, thinly sliced

Method

1. Cut the lavash into 8 pieces after preparing it according to the instructions. It's possible to make the lavash up to 4 days before the due date.
2. Place the lavash in a medium dish and set them upright to create height. Place the bowl on the board's top left corner, with any pieces that didn't fit in the bowl underneath it.
3. Place the smoked salmon slices in the bottom right corner, slightly overlapping them to add volume.
4. In the bottom left corner, place a tiny dish filled with cream cheese. With the handle sticking up, place the spreading knife in the cream cheese. Sprinkle some dill and chives on top of the cream cheese. Close the space between the cream cheese and salmon with the leftover dill on the right side of the bowl.
5. Arrange the tomatoes in the top right corner of the board, with the vines still attached.
6. Toss the capers with a tiny spoon in a small bowl and set next to the tomatoes.
7. Place the onion pieces evenly between the salmon and under the tomatoes.

Serving Suggestions: Grapefruit mimosas make a great sweet-tart pairing for this brunch.

30 Mins

0 Mins

4

Chapter 4

Large Boards

SORRENTO SUMMER SOLSTICE

INGREDIENTS

- 2 Artisan Focaccias
- 2 cups of Fresh Ricotta
- 1 cup of Olive Tapenade
- 2 cups of Pan-Roasted Garlic Almonds
- 6 ounces of taleggio (or brie or fontina)
- 5 ounces of casalingo salami (or any mild salami), thinly sliced
- 5 ounces of soppressata (or pepperoni), sliced
- 6 ounces of Parma ham, sliced

- 4 ounces of fig jam
- 1 bunch of green grapes
- 1 bunch of red grapes
- 1 pint of blackberries
- 1 pint of cherries
- 16 grissini sticks
- 6 ounces of black pepper crackers

directions :

1. Follow the recipes for the handmade focaccias, fresh ricotta, olive tapenade, and almonds.
2. Place a teaspoon of fresh ricotta in a medium mixing dish. Place it slightly to the right of the board's center.
3. Using a cheese knife, cut the taleggio into large pieces and arrange them in the upper left corner of the board.
4. Arrange the pieces of casalingo salami in the bottom left corner. Place the slices of soppressata in the bottom right corner. In the upper right corner, fold the Parma ham in ruffled layers.
5. In a small dish, place a heaping cup of tapenade and a small spoon, and place it over the casalingo salami.
6. Arrange the garlic almonds around the tapenade bowl.
7. Tuck the fig jam next to the Parma ham on the top right in a small dish with a small teaspoon peeking out of it.
8. Cut the grapes into little bunches and place them in any three available areas around the board. To add dimension to the board, scatter the blackberries over all of the grape heaps. The cherries should be placed on top of the grapes and blackberries.
9. Tear the focaccias into little pieces with your hands. With the focaccia, grissini sticks, and black pepper crackers, fill in the open spots on the board.

Serving Suggestions: Spumante Brut Rosé, a fruity and flowery Italian type with a touch of bubbles, is a superb choice.

2 hrs

0 Mins

8

NEW YEARS EVE

- 2½ pounds of fingerling potatoes
- 1 tablespoon of butter
- Sea salt
- Freshly ground black pepper
- 10 ounces of prosciutto, thinly sliced
- 10 ounces of salami, thinly sliced
- 1 (16-ounce) jar pickled pearl onions, drained
- 1 (13.5-ounce) jar cornichons, drained
- 12 ounces of raclette, sliced ¼-inch thick

directions :

1. In a medium saucepan, cover the potatoes with water and let them boil over high heat. Cook the potatoes for about 25 minutes, or until fork-tender. Drain and place in a large mixing bowl. Sprinkle with pepper and salt after tossing in the butter. Arrange the potatoes in the center of the board and crush them with a fork one by one. Place a serving spoon next to the mound and pile them together.
2. Arrange the prosciutto slices in the top left corner of the board, with a small fork.
3. Using another small fork, place the salami slices to the right of the prosciutto.
4. In a small dish, arrange the pickled pearl onions and a small spoon in the bottom left corner.
5. Using a small fork, place the cornichons in the bottom right corner of another small bowl.
6. In a nonstick saucepan, cook the raclette slices over medium-high heat for about 5 minutes or until completely melted. When the cheese is melted, it will have a nutty Swiss cheese scent.
7. Now for the fun part: smother the mashed potatoes in cheese in front of your visitors!

Serving Suggestions: A crisp, dry white wine is perfect for balancing the richness of the cured meats and raclette. You can select your favorite variety, but I highly recommend a Swiss Chasselas or an Austrian Riesling to keep things local.

15 Mins

25 Mins

8

THREE KINGS DAY

INGREDIENTS

- 4 (6.5-ounce) packages mini chorizo (we like Palacios)
- 8 ounces of jamón serrano (or prosciutto), thinly sliced
- 8 ounces of lomo (or Italian lardo), sliced
- 7½ ounces of Monte Enebro (or any blue cheese)
- 8 ounces of cabra romero (or any goat cheese)
- 8 ounces of Manchego (or any mild sheep milk cheese)
- 10 ounces of quince paste
- 1 pint of blackberries
- 2 pears, cored and thinly sliced
- 2 baguettes, cut into 2-inch slices

directions :

1. Arrange the mini chorizos in a small bowl, ready to be grabbed. Place the bowl on the board's top right corner.
2. Arrange the serrano jamón slices at the bottom middle of the board. Place the lomo slices in the upper left corner.
3. Using a cheese knife, lay the Monte Enebro slice below the lomo.
4. Using another cheese knife, place the cabra romero in the upper middle.
5. Remove roughly a quarter of a cup of pieces from the Manchego wedge. Arrange them with a cheese knife and the remaining Manchego slice in the top right region near the chorizo.
6. Place the quince paste cube above and to the right of the jamón serrano, in the middle of the board, with a small spreading knife.
7. Put blackberries in a medium bowl and place them near the Monte Enebro. Any leftover berries should be scattered about the bowl on the board.
8. Arrange the pear slices on the left side of the board in an empty area.
9. To fill in the gaps, place the baguette slices around the board in a few blank spots.

Serving Suggestions: This board looks great with the red undertones of Garnacha.

15 Mins

0 Mins

8

GERMAN SMOKED CHARCUTERIE

 INGREDIENTS

- 2 cups of Pickled Red Onion and Fennel
- 1 pound of bratwurst
- 2 tablespoons of olive oil
- 1 pound of knackwurst
- 16 ounces of beer cheese (or pub cheese)
- ¼ cup of yellow mustard
- 2 sourdough boules or loaves, cut or torn into large chunks

 directions :

1. Preheat the grill to medium-high. Grill the bratwurst for 15 minutes, tossing to sear both sides. Allow the grill to rest for 5 minutes on a chopping board. Cut into 1 or 2 inches pieces at a 45-degree angle and place with a fork in the correct center of the board.

2. In a medium skillet, heat the oil over medium-high heat. Cook for 15 minutes, turning the knackwurst to char on both sides, until golden brown and crispy. Allow it to rest for 5 minutes on a chopping board. Slice into 1 or 2-inch pieces at a 45-degree angle and arrange with a fork down the left-center of the board.

3. Place the beer cheese in the center of the board, between the two types of wurst, in a medium bowl. In the bowl, put a spoon.

4. Place the beer cheese in the center of the board, between the two types of wurst, in a medium bowl. In the bowl, put a spoon.

5. Combine the pickled red onion and fennel in a small bowl. Using a fork, place it underneath and to the left of the beer cheese.

6. Using a small spreading knife, put the mustard in a small dish in the upper right corner of the board.

7. Arrange the sourdough chunks along the board's outside edges.

Serving Suggestions: Try Weihenstephaner Pilsner, a light, crisp, transparent beer with a mild malty taste and an earthy scent of hops.

40 Mins

0 Mins

8

MOROCCAN MEZZE

- 3 cups of Goat Cheese Hummus
- 2 cups of Moroccan Spiced Chickpeas
- Extra-virgin olive oil
- 2 teaspoons of Moroccan spice blend
- 8 ounces of beef jerky (preferably peppered)
- 8 ounces of turkey jerky (preferably cured)
- 8 flatbreads
- ½ cup (1 stick) of unsalted butter
- 1 garlic clove, finely grated
- ¼ cup of chopped fresh parsley
- 16 dates (preferably Medjool)

 directions :

1. Toss the hummus with extra-virgin olive oil and a pinch of the Moroccan spice blend in a medium mixing bowl. Place a teaspoon next to the hummus bowl in the center of the board.

2. Arrange the Moroccan spiced chickpeas above and to the right of the hummus dish in a small bowl.

3. Sprinkle the remaining spice combination over the beef and turkey jerky in the upper left corner of the board.

4. Preheat the oven to 350°F. Set the flatbreads on a baking sheet with a rim. Melt the butter in a pan over high heat. Cook, stirring constantly, for 5 minutes, or until the butter has slightly browned.

5. Brush the flatbreads with the garlic butter and equally sprinkle the chopped parsley on top. Toast in the oven for 7 to 10 minutes, until the edges are golden. Cut into pieces and place them surrounding the hummus bowl.

6. Place the dates in the bottom right corner.

Serving Suggestions: Serve with mint green tea and a garnish of fresh mint leaves.

35 Mins

0 Mins

8

RUSTIC ROOTS

INGREDIENTS

- 1 pint of Spicy Dilly Beans
- 4 cups of Pan-Roasted Garlic Almonds
- 4 cups of Creamy Herb Yogurt Sauce
- 3 cups of Crispy Cauliflower
- 1 pound of rainbow carrots, peeled and cut into 3- to 4-inch sticks
- 2 bunches of small red radishes

- 5 ounces of salami, sliced
- 5 ounces of speck, sliced
- 2 cups of plantain chips
- 1 bag of tricolored root vegetable chips

directions :

1. Follow the recipes for preparing the dilly beans, pan-roasted garlic almonds, creamy herb yogurt sauce, and crispy cauliflower.
2. In the bottom right corner of the board, stand the dilly beans upright in a jar or medium bowl with high edges.
3. In a small bowl, place the pan-roasted garlic almonds in the bottom left corner.
4. Using a small spoon, spoon the creamy herb yogurt sauce into a medium bowl and place it in the upper left corner.
5. Arrange the crispy cauliflower florets in the board's center, cascading down to the bottom.
6. Place the rainbow carrots next to the herb yogurt sauce on a plate.
7. Arrange the radishes in a row to the right of the sauce.
8. Using tongs, arrange the salami and speck pieces in the upper right corner.
9. Arrange the plantain chips on top of the charcuterie in the empty area.
10. Scatter the tricolored root vegetable chips around the edges, filling in any blank spaces.

Serving Suggestions: Pinot Grigio pairs well with this board

2 hrs 12 Mins

0 Mins

8

SPANISH SEABOARD

INGREDIENTS

- 1½ cups of Chimichurri
- 12 Roasted Vine Campari Tomatoes
- 1½ pounds of Yukon Gold potatoes, quartered
- ¼ cup plus 2 tablespoons of extra-virgin olive oil, divided
- 1 teaspoon of sea salt, plus more to season
- Freshly ground black pepper
- 1 pound of octopus tentacles

- ½ cup (1 stick) of unsalted butter
- 5 garlic cloves, peeled
- 1 pound of large shrimp, peeled and deveined
- 10 ounces of Mahón (or any mild cow milk cheese)
- 1 (12-ounce) jar pickled hot peppers, drained

directions :

1. Preheat the oven to 375°F. Add ¼ cup olive oil, 1 teaspoon sea salt, and a little black pepper to the potatoes on a rimmed baking sheet. Heat the potatoes for 40 minutes, or until crispy, golden brown, and fork-tender. Season the crispy potatoes with sea salt and pepper and place them in the top right corner of the board.
2. Heat a grill or a large skillet to high temperatures. The octopus tentacles should be charred for 3 to 4 minutes, turning once. Place on the upper left side of the board, cut into ½-inch pieces. Sprinkle the remaining 2 tablespoons of olive oil over the top and season with salt and pepper.
3. Drizzle a little chimichurri on top of the octopus. Place the remaining ingredients in a small dish with a little spoon beneath the octopus.
5. In a large skillet, melt the butter and garlic over medium-high heat. Sauté the shrimp in the garlic butter until completely pink, about 5 minutes, turning once halfway through. Move the shrimp to a medium bowl with a slotted spoon and arrange in the center of the board.
6. In the bottom left corner, arrange the roasted tomatoes.
7. Using a cheese knife, place the Mahón cheese in the bottom right corner of the board.
8. In the middle right corner, place the pickled spicy peppers.

Serving Suggestions: Bodegas Muga Seleccion is a Spanish red wine that will complements this board

35 Mins

0 Mins

8

GOLDEN CELEBRATION

INGREDIENTS

- 2 (8-ounce) wheels Camembert
- 1 cup of caramel sauce
- 1 cup of roasted pecans
- Sea salt
- 5½ ounces of truffle salami (we like Creminelli Tartufo Salami), thinly sliced

- 4 Bosc pears, cored and sliced
- 8 fresh figs, cut in half
- 1 pint of fresh white currants (or Rainiercherries)
- 1 choolate babka
- 1 baguette

directions :

1. Preheat the oven to 350°F. Place the two wheels of Camembert cheese on a rimmed baking sheet lined with parchment paper. Bake for about 20 minutes, or until the cheese in the center is soft and melted.
2. Remove from the oven and place in the center of your serving board.
3. In a small saucepan, gently reheat the caramel sauce until it's runny, then ladle it over the cheese. Serve with a generous handful of toasted nuts and a sprinkling of sea salt on top.
4. Arrange the salami slices at the board's right bottom.
5. Arrange the pear slices from top to bottom on the right side of the board.
6. Arrange the fig halves around the pears and salami.
7. Arrange the salami on top of the white currants.
8. Cut half of the chocolate babka into slices and arrange them in the top left corner of the board, along with the remaining bread. Next to the loaf, place a bread knife.
9. Tear the baguette into large chunks and arrange them in the bottom left corner.

Serving Suggestions: For an equally decadent refreshment, try a soixante-quinze.

15 Mins

20 Mins

8

DOLCE MILAN

 INGREDIENTS

- 1 cup of Meyer Lemon Marmalade
- 7 ounces of stracchino (or ricotta)
- 5½ ounces of Milano salami, thinly sliced
- 12 ounces of Iberian shoulder ham (or any mild ham), thinly sliced
- 1 loaf of panettone (or fruit bread or brioche)

- ½ cup (1 stick) of unsalted butter, melted
- Confectioners' sugar, for dusting
- 1 pint of fresh figs, halved
- 1 pint of blackberries
- 1 pint of blueberries

 directions :

1. In the top left corner, but away from the board's edge, place the stracchino cheese in a tiny dish with a spoon next to it.
2. Arrange the Milano salami slices in the upper right corner of the board, near the stracchino.
3. Place the Iberian ham slices in the centre right corner of the board.
4. Preheat the oven to 375°F. Arrange the panettone slices on a rimmed baking sheet and spread them lightly with melted butter on both sides. Toast for 3 to 5 minutes in the oven, until golden and browned around the edges. Place the slices on the board's middle, shingling from left to right. Confectioners' sugar is sprinkled on top.
5. Using a small spoon, place the Meyer lemon marmalade in a small dish or jar in the bottom right corner of the board.
6. Place the fig halves in the bottom left corner.
7. Pile the blackberries with the figs but cascading toward the center of the board.
8. Sprinkle the figs and blackberries with the blueberries.

Serving Suggestions: A great pairing for this board would be a Lombardian red wine such as Valtellina

35 Mins

0 Mins

8

A NIGHT IN

INGREDIENTS

- 2 cups of Pan-Roasted Garlic Almonds
- 4 ounces of Jarlsberg
- 4 ounces of smoked Gouda
- 4 ounces of Dubliner
- 5 ounces of salami, thinly sliced
- 5 ounces of Tuscan salami, thinly sliced
- 5 ounces of spicy salami, thinly sliced
- 1 bunch of red grapes
- 1 bunch of green grapes
- 1 pint of raspberries
- 1 cup of dried apricots
- 1 traditional baguette, sliced
- 1 sourdough baguette, sliced

directions :

1. Half of the Jarlsberg wedge should be cut into tiny pieces. Using a cheese knife, place the remaining wedge in the top left corner of the board and surround it with the smaller pieces.
2. Using a cheese knife, place the Gouda in the bottom right corner.
3. Crumble the Dubliner into bite-sized pieces and stack them on the board's bottom left corner.
4. Arrange the standard and Tuscan salami slices above the Gouda, from the centre to the right side of the board. Arrange the spicy salami slices on the board's bottom middle area.
5. To add height to the board, cut the red and green grapes into little bunches and arrange them in the center. Fill in a few holes on both sides of the board by cascading some down either side. Sprinkle the raspberries over the grapes.
6. To add height to the board, cut the red and green grapes into little bunches and arrange them in the center. Fill in a few spaces on both sides of the board by cascading some down either side. Sprinkle the raspberries over the grapes.
7. Place the dried apricots in the bottom right corner of the board.
8. On the left side, place a small bowl of almonds alongside some grape bunches.
9. Fill any empty places with a few pieces of baguette, and serve the rest in a big dish on the side.

Serving Suggestions: Make a cara cara mojito, a sweet, citrusy, herbal drink with just the proper amount of bubbles, for a wonderfully lively beverage.

15 Mins

0 Mins

8

Chapter 5

Preserves, Spreads, Dips, and Condiments

Easy Butterscotch Sauce

 INGREDIENTS

- ½ cup of unsalted butter
- 1 cup of packed brown sugar
- 1 cup of heavy cream
- About ½ teaspoon of regular salt
- About 1 tablespoon of vanilla extract
- 2 tablespoons of bourbon (optional)

Method

1. Melt the butter in a large medium pot over medium heat.
2. Pour in the sugar and whisk to combine. It will appear sandy at first, but keep an eye out for when the sugar has completely dissolved.
3. Add the cream and whisk it in after the sugar has dissolved. Cook, stirring often until the temperature reaches 225°F.
4. Remove the pot from the heat and set it aside to cool before seasoning with salt and vanilla. Add little quantities at a time and taste as you go. 5. If you're using bourbon, pour it in now.
6. Transfer the sauce to mason jars and seal them. Refrigerate.

10 Mins

40 Mins

3

Hot Fudge Sauce

 **INGREDIENTS**

- 2 cups of chocolate chips (your choice, but semi-sweet is what we use)
- ¾ cup of granulated sugar
- 1 (12-ounce) can of evaporated milk
- 2 tablespoons of unsalted butter
- 1 ½ teaspoons of vanilla extract
- ½ teaspoon of salt

Method

1. Add the chocolate, sugar, evaporated milk, and butter in a large saucepan over medium heat.
2. Cook for 5 minutes, or until all of ingredients have melted.
3. Bring it to a mild boil, stirring frequently, then remove it from the heat. Combine the vanilla and salt in a mixing bowl.
4. Pour it into mason jars and set aside to thicken as it cools.
5. Microwave for 30 seconds at a time to reheat.

10 Mins

10 Mins

3

Rum and Butter Sauce

 INGREDIENTS

- ¾ cup of unsalted butter
- 1 ½ cups of light brown sugar
- ⅔ cup of heavy cream
- 6 tablespoons of dark rum
- 2 teaspoons of vanilla
- Flaked sea salt
- ½ cup of sultana raisins (optional)

Method

1. Preheat a skillet to medium-high heat.
2. Melt the butter in a large mixing bowl and stir in the brown sugar until thoroughly combined. Drizzle in the cream, rum, and vanilla extract while stirring.
3. Cook for another 5 minutes, stirring occasionally, before removing the pan from the heat and allowing it to cool.
4. Fill the bottles with the mixture and seal them. Refrigerate for up to 2 weeks before serving.

10 Mins

10 Mins

3

Vanilla Cream Sauce

 **INGREDIENTS**

- 2 cups of heavy cream
- 1 cup of granulated sugar
- 2 tablespoons of cornstarch
- ½ cup of unsalted butter
- 1 ½ teaspoon of vanilla extract
- ½ teaspoon of salt

Method

1. Mix the cream, sugar, cornstarch, and butter in a heavy medium saucepan over medium heat. Cook, stirring constantly until the sauce has thickened and is bubbling.
2. Bring to a low boil for 3 minutes, then remove from the heat and stir in the vanilla and salt.
3. Remove the sauce from the heat and place it in mason jars to cool.
4. Refrigerate for up to 2 weeks before eating.

10Mins

20 Mins

3

Pineapple Ginger Sauce

 INGREDIENTS

- 1 cup of pineapple juice
- ½ cup of orange marmalade
- 1 tablespoon of fresh ginger, minced
- 1 tablespoon of cornstarch

Method

1. In a large saucepan over medium heat, mix all the ingredients and cook until bubbling and thick.
2. Remove the sauce from the heat and place it in mason jars to cool.
3. Keep refrigerated and consume within three weeks.

10 Mins

40 Mins

3

Fireball Whisky Sauce

 INGREDIENTS

- 2 cups of light brown sugar
- 1 cup of butter
- 1 cup of heavy cream
- ¾ teaspoon of salt
- ½ cup of Fireball Cinnamon Whisky

Method

1. In a medium saucepan, mix the sugar, butter, cream, and salt. Cook for 5 minutes, or until all ingredients have melted together.
2. Stir in the whiskey and boil for another 10 minutes, or until the sauce thickens.
3. Remove the pot from the heat and let it cool gradually. Fill clean jars with it and seal them.
4. If it lasts that long, keep it in the fridge for up to 2 weeks.

7 Mins

15 Mins

3

An Italian Date

- 5½ ounces of speck, thinly sliced
- 10 ounces of Salami Picante
- 8 ounces of pecorino, sliced
- ¼ cup of honey
- 2 (6-ounce) fresh Mozzarella balls
- 2 tablespoons of chili oil
- Sea salt
- Freshly ground black pepper
- 1 (12-inch) Neapolitan-style flatbread, pizza crust, or focaccia
- 1½ cups of arugula
- Extra-virgin olive oil for drizzling
- You will also need: a large board, a small knife, a small jar or dish, a honey wand or spoon, 2 cheese knives

Method

1. Arrange the sliced speck on a large board in the upper left corner.
2. Cut half of the Salami Picante into slices and arrange the pieces on the top center of the board, near the speck, with a small knife.
3. Arrange the pecorino pieces beneath the salami.
4. Place the honey in a tiny jar to the right of the pecorino, using a honey wand or spoon.
5. Arrange the mozzarella balls in the board's bottom right corner.
6. Season the cheese with sea salt and pepper after drizzling it with chile oil. Beside it, place two cheese forks.
7. Layer the flatbread to the left of the mozzarella down the bottom of the board in 2-by-5-inch rectangles.

10 Mins

40 Mins

3

Chapter 6

Special Occasions

Boards

INGREDIENTS

- 2 tablespoons of butter
- ½ pound of lean ground beef
- Salt and pepper to taste
- 1 teaspoon of dried basil
- ½ pound of iceberg lettuce
- ½ cup of cheddar cheese, diced
- ¼ cup of grated parmesan cheese
- Dressing
- 3 tablespoons of olive oil
- 1 tablespoon of Dijon mustard
- ¼ cup mayonnaise
- Salt and pepper to taste
- Zest of 1 lemon
- 2 tablespoons of freshly chopped mint

10 Mins

50 Mins

4

Cheesy Ground Beef Salad

directions :

1. In a large skillet, heat the oil and add the ground beef.
2. Add salt, pepper, and basil to taste. Allow to cool fully before serving.
3. Arrange the lettuce with the chilled ground beef, cheddar, and parmesan in a salad dish.
4. In a jar, combine the olive oil, Dijon mustard, mayonnaise, salt & pepper, lemon peel, and fresh mint. Serve.

Nutrition:
- Calories 340
- Fat 20.4
- Fiber 6.6
- Carbs 22.3
- Protein 18.

 10 Mins   40 Mins   5

Orange Ponzu

 directions :

1. In a saucepan, combine the orange quarters, konbu, bonito shavings, rice vinegar, and soy sauce. Allow for a half-hour of standing time.
2. Boil the mixture. Take it away from the heat once it begins to boil.
3. Allow it to cool before straining through a cheesecloth-lined strainer.

 INGREDIENTS

- 1/4 cup of soy sauce
- 1/2 cup of rice vinegar
- 2 tablespoons of bonito shavings (dry fish flakes)
- 1 (1 inch) square kombu (kelp)
- 1 orange, quartered

INGREDIENTS

- 2 tablespoons of butter
- ½ pound of ground sirloin
- Salt and pepper to taste
- 1 teaspoon of dried dill
- ½ pound of baby spinach
- 1 cup of diced strawberries
- ¼ cup of grated parmesan cheese
- 1 cup of mozzarella balls
- Dressing
- 3 tablespoons of olive oil
- 1 tablespoon of Dijon mustard
- 2 tablespoons of balsamic vinegar
- Salt and pepper to taste

 10 Mins

 40 Mins

 4

Baby Spinach and Ground Beef Salad

 directions :

1. Heat the oil in a nonstick frying pan.
2. Add the ground beef to the pan.
3. Add salt, pepper, and dill to taste. Allow to cool fully before serving.
4. Toss the baby spinach with the chilled ground beef, cut strawberries, parmesan, and mozzarella balls in a salad dish.
5. In a jar, combine the olive oil, Dijon mustard, balsamic vinegar, salt, and pepper.

Nutrition:
- Calories 340
- Fat 20.7
- Fiber 7
- Carbs 28.9
- Protein 12.5.

- 2 tablespoons of butter
- ½ pound of ground sirloin
- Salt and pepper to taste
- 1 teaspoon of dried parsley
- ½ pound of lettuce
- ½ cup of chopped walnuts
- ¼ cup of grated parmesan cheese
- 1 cup of mozzarella balls
- Dressing
- 3 tablespoons of olive oil
- 1 tablespoon of Dijon mustard
- 3 tablespoons of mayonnaise
- 2 tablespoons of cream cheese
- Salt and pepper to taste
- 1 teaspoon of chili flakes

10 Mins

40 Mins

2

Cesar Ground Beef Salad

 directions :

1. Heat the oil in a nonstick frying pan. Add the ground beef to the pan.
2. Add salt, pepper, and parsley to taste.
3. Set aside to cool fully.
4. Toss the lettuce with chilled ground beef, walnuts, parmesan, and mozzarella balls in a salad dish.
5. In a jar, combine the olive oil, Dijon mustard, mayonnaise, and cream cheese, seasoning to taste with salt and pepper.
Serve

Nutrition:

- Calories 340
- Fat 20.4
- Fiber 6.6
- Carbs 22.3
- Protein 18.8.

 INGREDIENTS

- 2 tablespoons of olive oil
- ½ pound of ground sirloin
- Salt and pepper to taste
- 1 teaspoon of curry powder
- ½ pound of lettuce, chopped
- ¾ cup of chopped almonds
- ¼ cup of grated parmesan cheese
- 2 hard boiled eggs, chopped
- Dressing
- 3 tablespoons of olive oil
- 1 tablespoon of Dijon mustard
- 3 tablespoons of mayonnaise
- ½ cup of cream cheese
- ½ cup of sour cream
- Salt and pepper to taste
- 1 teaspoon of chili flakes

10 Mins

120 Mins

2

Creamy Almond and Ground Beef Salad

 directions :

1. Melt the butter in a nonstick frying pan. Add the ground beef to the pan.
2. Add salt, pepper, and curry powder to taste.
3. Set aside to cool fully.
4. Toss the lettuce with chilled ground beef, almonds, parmesan, and cooked eggs in a salad dish.
5. Season with salt, pepper, and chili flakes then mix the olive oil, Dijon mustard, mayonnaise, cream cheese, and sour cream in a jar.
Serve

INGREDIENTS

- 2 cups of crumbled cornbread
- 10 oz. of can enchilada sauce
- ½ teaspoon of salt
- 1 ½ lbs. of ground beef
- 1 ½ cups of salsa

10 Mins

30 Mins

4

Enchilada Meatballs

 directions :

1. In a mixing bowl, mix the cornmeal, enchilada sauce, salt, and ground meat.
2. Mix with your hands until everything is fully blended. Make 1inch meatballs out of the meat.
3. Preheat the oven to 350 ℉. In a large baking pan, place the meatballs.
4. Bake for 12 minutes, or until the meatballs are thoroughly browned and no longer pink.
5. Before serving, remove the meatballs from the oven and drain them on paper towels.
6. Transfer the meatballs to a serving dish.
7. Toss the meatballs in the salsa and serve.

Nutrition:

- Calories 360
- Fat 22.9
- Fiber 0.8
- Carbs 2.9
- Protein 33.6.

INGREDIENTS

- 2 cups of crumbled cornbread
- 10 oz. of can enchilada sauce
- ½ teaspoon of salt
- 1 ½ lbs. of ground beef
- 1 ½ cups of salsa

10 Mins

30 Mins

8

Hamburger Broccoli Dip

 directions :

1. In a medium-sized skillet, season the ground beef with a pinch of salt.
2. As the ground beef cooks, stir regularly to break it up into crumbles.
3. Cook, stirring occasionally, for approximately 5 minutes, or until the ground beef is nicely browned and no longer pink. Remove the skillet from the heat and drain all of the oil.
4. Add the broccoli, Velveeta cheese, and Rotel tomatoes into the skillet.
5. Cook, stirring regularly, until the cheese has melted and the dip has heated through.
6. Remove the dip from the skillet and place it in a serving dish.
7. Mix the dip with corn chips and serve.

INGREDIENTS

- 4 slices bread
- 1 1/4 cups of chopped onion
- 1/2 cup of chopped green bell pepper
- 1 lb. of lean ground beef
- 1/2 lb. of lean ground pork
- 2 eggs, beaten
- 10 oz. of can Rotel tomatoes
- 3/4 teaspoon of salt

15 Mins

30 Mins

6

Southwestern Classic

 directions :

1. Place the bread in a food processor. Process until relatively small crumbs form.
2. Place the crumbs in a mixing dish and stir to combine.
3. In a large mixing bowl, combine the chopped onion, green bell pepper, ground beef, pork, eggs, Rotel tomatoes with juice, and salt.
4. Mix with your hands until everything is fully blended. There will be no firmness in the mixture.
5. Form the meat into a 12-inch loaf.
6. Place the bread on a broiler pan and broil until golden brown.
7. Preheat the oven to 375 °F.
8. Cover the meatloaf loosely with aluminum foil. Bake for 1 hour in the oven.
9. Remove the aluminum foil and bake the meatloaf for 30 minutes, or until it is no longer pink, firm, and done.
10. Take the meatloaf out of the oven and set it aside to cool for 5 minutes before slicing.

INGREDIENTS

- 8 frozen mochi squares
- 1/2 cup of soy sauce
- 1 sheet nori (dry seaweed)

10 Mins

40 Mins

5

Broiled Mochi with Nori Seaweed

directions :

1. Preheat the oven to 450 °F.
2. Place the mochi on a baking sheet after dipping it in the soy sauce.
3. Bake for about five minutes, or until well heated.
4. Slice dry seaweed into eight strips as the mochi cooks. Place these strips into a large frying pan on medium heat. After 1 to 2 minutes of warming, remove them from the heat.
5. Use seaweed to wrap each mochi cake and serve warm.

 INGREDIENTS

- 1 cup of uncooked white rice
- 2 cups of water
- 2 tablespoons of rice vinegar
- 1 teaspoon of salt
- 2 sheets of nori seaweed sheets
- 1/4 cucumber, peeled and sliced lengthwise
- 2 pieces imitation crab legs
- 1/2 (3 ounces) package cream cheese, sliced
- 1 teaspoon of minced fresh ginger root

 10 Mins

 40 Mins

 5

Cream Cheese and Crab Sushi Rolls

 directions :

1. Boil water and rice in a saucepan over high heat. Reduce heat to medium-low, cover, and cook for 20 to 25 minutes, or until rice is cooked and liquid has been absorbed. Mix the salt and rice vinegar in a mixing bowl. Allow it to cool completely.
2. Lay down the seaweed sheets. Wet your hands with water, then evenly distribute rice on each sheet, leaving a half-inch gap along each longitudinal edge.
3. Arrange cream cheese, imitation crab meat, and cucumber slices in a straight line across the other side of the area.
4. Begin rolling sushi from the toppings to the uncovered end of the seaweed sheet.
5. Using a sharp wet knife, cut each roll into 5 or 6 sections. Serve with ginger chopped on the side.

Chapter 7

Nuts, Olives, and Pickles

Baked French Brie with Peaches, Pecans, and Honey

INGREDIENTS

- 1 (9") wheel of French Brie
- 1 (15 ounces) can of peaches (cubed)
- ¼ cup of pecans (crushed)
- 5 sprigs of fresh thyme
- 3 basil leaves (finely sliced)
- Runny honey (as needed)
- French baguette (sliced, to serve)

directions :

1. Preheat the oven to 425 °F.
2. Place the Brie in an oven-safe ceramic dish, unwrapped.
3. Add the peach cubes on top.
4. Sprinkle the pecans on top.
5. Spray with honey and sprinkle with thyme and basil.
6. Bake for 15-20 minutes in a preheated oven or until the cheese is completely melted and lightly colored.
7. Serve with fresh French baguette slices.

10 Mins

20 Mins

3

Macadamia Nut Hummus

INGREDIENTS

- 3 cloves garlic
- 2 cups ofcanned chickpeas (drained, liquid reserved)
- 1½ teaspoon salt
- ¼ cup tahini
- 5 tablespoons freshly squeezed lemon juice
- 2 tablespoons chickpea liquid
- ½ cup roasted macadamia nuts
- Olive oil (to drizzle)

directions :

1. While the food blender is operating, add the garlic through the cover and blend until minced.
2. Blend until smooth with chickpeas, salt, tahini, lemon juice, chickpea liquid, and macadamia nuts.
3. Serve with a drizzle of olive oil.

10 Mins

10 Mins

3

Pistachio-Crusted Shrimp with Orange Zest

 INGREDIENTS

- 20-24 jumbo shrimp (shelled, deveined)
- 1 cup of pistachios (coarsely ground)
- 2 small eggs
- 4 tablespoons of virgin olive oil
- Sea salt
- Zest of 1 orange

directions :

1. Using kitchen paper towels, pat the shrimp dry.
2. Place the pistachios in a large mixing bowl.
3. Lightly whisk the eggs in a separate large mixing dish.
4. Dip the shrimp in the eggs in batches, shaking off any excess.
5. Sprinkle with ground pistachios, shaking off any excess.
6. Continue until all the shrimp are covered.
7. Heat the oil in a pan over medium heat.
8. Cook the shrimp for 3-4 minutes on each side in the heated oil or until fully done.
9. Season with salt and orange zest when ready to serve, and enjoy.

10 Mins

30 Mins

4

Spanish Almond Soup

- I cup of blanched slivered almonds
- 1 clove of garlic (peeled)
- 2 cups of cold filtered water
- 1 cup of fresh bread (crusts removed, cubed)
- 1 tablespoon of sherry vinegar
- 1 tablespoon of extra-virgin olive oil
- Salt and freshly ground pepper (to taste)
- Olive oil (to serve)
- Mint leaves (to serve)
- Toasted almonds (to serve)

directions :

1. Combine the almonds, garlic, and cold water in a food processor and process until completely creamy and smooth.
2. The mixture must be strained through a fine-mesh sieve. Slowly increase the speed of the blender before increasing it to high.
3. Add the bread chunks and purée until smooth once more.
4. Season with salt and pepper to taste after adding the sherry vinegar and oil.
5. Refrigerate for at least 2 hours after transferring to an airtight container.
6. Serve chilled after stirring, drizzling with oil, and topping up with mint leaves and toasted almonds.

10 Mins

160 Mins

3

Tomato, Raisin, and Pine Nut Bruschetta

INGREDIENTS

- 2 tablespoons of extra-virgin olive oil
- 1 large shallot (minced)
- 1 small dried red pepper (seeded, chopped)
- 2 cups of cherry tomatoes (washed, cut into quarters)
- Sea salt (to season)
- ½ cup of pine nuts
- ½ cup of raisins
- 12 (½") slices of ciabatta
- Olive oil (to brush)

directions :

1. Heat the oil over moderately high heat until it begins to ripple.
2. Add the shallots to the pan, along with the dried red pepper, and cook, turning constantly, until the shallots are transparent.
3. Add the tomatoes and a pinch of salt after that.
4. Lower the heat to low and cook for 10-15 minutes, or until the sauce has thickened somewhat and the tomatoes have turned a rich orange-red color. Combine the pine nuts and raisins in a mixing bowl.
5. Cook for a further 10-15 minutes, stirring regularly, to enable the raisins to plump and the sauce to thicken.
6. Season with salt and pepper, taste, and leave aside to cool somewhat.
7. Brush a drop of olive oil over the ciabatta pieces and toast on both sides. Toss the tomato mixture on top of the toasted bread and serve.

10 Mins

40 Mins

3

Tropical Chicken Salad

INGREDIENTS

- 2 cups of cooked deli chicken (cubed)
- 1 cup of celery (trimmed, chopped)
- 1 cup mayonnaise
- ½ - 1 teaspoon of curry powder (to taste)
- 1 (20 ounces) can of pineapple chunks (drained)
- 2 large-size firm bananas (peeled, sliced)
- 1 (11 ounces) can mandarin orange (drained)
- ½ cup of sweetened coconut (shredded)
- Salad greens (optional)
- ¾ cup of salted cashews or peanuts

directions :

1. In a mixing dish, combine the chicken and celery.
2. Mix the mayonnaise and curry powder (to taste) in a large mixing bowl.
3. Refrigerate for at least half an hour after covering with a lid. When you are ready to serve, gently mix the pineapple pieces, banana, mandarin orange, and shredded coconut.
4. Arrange on top of fresh salad leaves and top with nuts.

10 Mins

40 Mins

3

Almond Crusted Cheesy

INGREDIENTS

- 1 cup of sliced almonds
- 8 ounces of cream cheese (softened)
- 2 ounces blue cheese (room temperature, crumbled)
- 2 tablespoons fresh parsley (minced)
- 2 tablespoons of heavy whipping cream (room temperature)
- 1-1¼ pounds of seedless red or green grapes (rinsed, patted dry)

directions :

1. Preheat the oven to 275 ℉.
2. Blend the almonds in a food processor until finely chopped.
3. In a 15x10x1inches baking tray, spread the chopped almonds and bake for 6-8 minutes, stirring regularly, until golden.
4. Place the mixture in a shallow basin and set aside to cool.
5. In a separate dish, mix the cream cheese, blue cheese, parsley, and whipping cream until smooth.
6. Place a cocktail stick in the center of each grape.
7. Roll the grapes, then the almonds, in the cheese mixture.
8. Place the grapes on waxed paper-lined baking pans.
9. Cover and place in the refrigerator until ready to serve.

10 Mins

20 Mins

3

Curried Tropical Nut Mix

 INGREDIENTS

- 2 tablespoons of curry powder
- 1 tablespoon of butter
- 1 tablespoon ofolive oil
- ½ teaspoon cayenne pepper
- 1 teaspoon ground cumin
- 6 cups of salted, mixed nuts
- 1 cup of shredded sweetened coconut
- ½ cup of dried mango (chopped)

directions :

1. Mix the curry powder, butter, olive oil, cayenne pepper, and powdered cumin in a microwave-safe bowl. Microwave on high for 30 seconds uncovered.
2. Add the cashews, almonds, peanuts, and shredded coconut until uniformly coated.
3. Cook for a further 5 minutes, uncovered, until gently browned, stirring often. Add the mangoes, chopped.
4. Spread the mixture out on wax paper to cool.
5. Store in a resealable, airtight container.

10 Mins

20 Mins

3

Pine Nut and Zucchini

INGREDIENTS

- ¼ cup of pine nuts
- 2 large zucchinis (grated)
- 2 scallions (finely chopped)
- ¼ cup of low-fat feta cheese
- 1½ cups wholemeal plain flour
- ¾ cup buttermilk
- 1 medium-size egg (lightly beaten)
- 1 tablespoon of flat-leaf parsley (chopped)
- 2 tablespoons of sweet chili sauce
- Nonstick cooking spray
- 4 wedges of lemon

directions :

1. In a large mixing bowl, combine the pine nuts, zucchini, scallions, feta cheese, plain flour, buttermilk, egg, parsley, and sweet chili sauce. Set aside for a minimum of 10 minutes.
2. Preheat a frying pan over medium heat and coat with nonstick cooking spray.
3. Drop the mixture into the pan by tablespoonfuls and cook for a few minutes on each side until brown and cooked through.
4. Carefully remove the fritters from the pan. While you finish the rest of the fritter batter, keep it warm.
5. Serve with a lemon slice as a garnish.

10 Mins

40 Mins

3

Roasted Almonds with Paprika

INGREDIENTS

- 1 cup of raw whole almonds
- 1 teaspoon of extra-virgin olive oil
- ½ teaspoon of smoked paprika
- ½ teaspoon flaky sea salt
- Zest of 1 medium orange

directions :

1. Preheat the oven to 325 °F. Use parchment paper to line a baking sheet. Place them to the side.
2. Mix the almonds with olive oil, smoked paprika, and sea salt in a mixing dish.
3. Evenly distribute the mixture on the baking sheet.
4. Place the nuts in the oven for 15 minutes, stirring every 4-5 minutes, until brown and aromatic.
5. Allow it to cool completely before tossing with the orange zest.
Enjoy.

10 Mins

40 Mins

3

Slow Cooker Candied Nuts

 INGREDIENTS

- ½ cup of butter (melted)
- ½ cup of powdered sugar
- 1 ½ teaspoon of ground cinnamon
- ¼ teaspoon of ground ginger
- ¼ teaspoon ground allspice
- 1½ cups of pecan halves
- 1½ cups of walnut halves
- 1 cup of unblanched almonds

directions :

1. Mix the butter, powdered sugar, ground cinnamon, ginger, and allspice in a greased 3-quart slow cooker.
2. Toss in the pecan and walnut halves to evenly coat them.
3. Cook on low, covered, for 2-3 hours, or until the nuts are crunchy.
4. During the cooking process, you will need to stir once.
5. Allow the nuts to cool fully on waxed paper.

10 Mins

30 Mins

3

Honey Mustard Nut Mix

 INGREDIENTS

- 2 egg whites
- ¼ cup of honey
- 2 tablespoons of stone-ground mustard
- 1 tablespoon of ground mustard powder
- 1 tablespoon Worcestershire sauce
- 3 cups raw mixed nuts (pistachios, almonds, pecans, and/or walnuts)
- 1 cup of large pretzels, roughly chopped
- 1 teaspoon of sea salt

 directions :

1. Preheat the oven to 225 ℉. Butter a large baking sheet that has been lined with foil.
2. In a mixing basin, whisk the egg whites together until slightly foamy. Combine the honey, mustard, mustard powder, and Worcestershire sauce in a large mixing bowl.
3. Toss in the nuts and pretzels to mix.
4. Bake for 45 minutes to 1 hour, stirring every 15 minutes, on the prepared baking sheet.
5. Season with salt and store in an airtight jar after cooling.

10 Mins

60 Mins

3

Chargrilled Lamb Cutlets with Macadamia Pesto

INGREDIENTS

- 3 cups of packed fresh basil leaves
- ½ cup of extra virgin olive oil (divided)
- 1 tablespoon of freshly squeezed lemon juice
- ¼ cup of raw macadamia nuts
- 1 large clove of garlic (peeled, crushed)
- Pinch of salt
- 12 lamb cutlets

directions :

1. Blend the basil leaves and ¼ cup of oil in a blender until finely minced.
2. Blend until smooth, adding the freshly squeezed lemon juice, macadamia nuts, garlic, salt, and the remaining olive oil.
3. Season with a little salt and pepper, if desired.
4. Cook the lamb cutlets for 3-4 minutes on each side, or until done to your liking.
5. Remove the lamb cutlets from the grill and toss them with the pesto before serving.

10 Mins

40 Mins

3

Cashew Nut and Pesto Pasta and Orange Grapes

 INGREDIENTS

- 7 ounces of fusilli pasta
- 10 Cashew nuts
- 2 garlic cloves (peeled)
- Sea salt and freshly ground black pepper
- squeezed juice of 1 lemon
- 2 handfuls of rocket leaves (washed, dried, chopped)
- Olive oil
- 2 tablespoons of Parmesan cheese (freshly grated)
- A handful of basil leaves (chopped)

 directions :

1. Cook the pasta until it is al dente, as directed on the package. Drain the water and keep it warm.
2. In the meantime, pound the nuts in a pestle and mortar to make a fine powder.
3. Toss in the garlic and a pinch of sea salt, and pound.
4. Pound and crush the mixture with the lemon zest and juice until it has a pesto-like consistency.
5. Stir in the grated Parmesan and enough oil to make a sauce.
Add extra salt and black pepper to taste, then toss in the heated pasta.

10 Mins

20 Mins

3

Trail Mix with Dark Chocolate and Toasted Coconut

 INGREDIENTS

- 1 cup of unsweetened coconut flakes
- 1 cup of raw almonds
- 1 cup of raw walnuts
- 1 cup of lightly salted, roasted cashews
- ½ cup of raw sunflower seeds
- 1 cup of dried cherries
- ¾ cup of dark chocolate chunks

 directions :

1. In a small frying pan on the stove, toast the coconut flakes over moderate-low heat, turning regularly, until fragrant and faintly brown. This will take around 2-3 minutes. It's important not to let the mixture cool.
2. In a large mixing bowl, add the toasted coconut, almonds, walnuts, cashews, sunflower seeds, cherries, and dark chocolate chips, stirring to mix.
3. Store in an airtight container.

10 Mins

40 Mins

3

Candied Pecans

- 2 cups of granulated sugar
- 1 ½ teaspoon of ground cinnamon
- 1 ½ teaspoons of salt
- 2 egg whites
- 2 tablespoons of water
- 2 pounds pecan halves

directions :

1. Preheat the oven to 250 ℉. Butter a large baking sheet that has been lined with foil.
2. Combine the sugar, cinnamon, and salt in a small bowl. Mix thoroughly.
3. Whisk the egg whites with the water in a large mixing basin until foamy.
4. Toss in the pecans, then whisk in the sugar mixture.
5. Mix everything thoroughly before spreading it out on the prepared baking sheet. Bake for 1 hour, stirring every 15 minutes until brown.

10 Mins

40 Mins

3

Swedish Nuts

INGREDIENTS

- ½ cup of butter
- 2 egg whites
- 1 cup of sugar
- 3-4 cups of raw pecans

directions :

1. Preheat oven to 350 °F.
2. Melt the butter in a 9x13-inch pan in the oven.
3. Whisk the egg whites until they are stiff.
4. Continue whisking the egg whites after adding the sugar.
5. Gently fold the nuts into the egg white-sugar mixture and arrange it evenly in the baking pan.
6. Bake the nuts for 30-40 minutes in the oven, stirring after the first 8-10 minutes. Stir every 4-5 minutes until everything is done. Allow it to cool before serving.
7. You'll need to keep stirring in the meantime, as the pecans cool.

10 Mins

40 Mins

5

Fruit and Nut White Clusters

 INGREDIENTS

- ½ cup of dried cranberries
- ½ cup of pumpkin seeds (hulls removed)
- ½ cup of sunflower seeds
- ½ cup of sliced cashews
- 2 cups of good quality white chocolate chips
- ½ teaspoon of sea salt

directions :

1. Line a baking sheet with foil and gently coat it with cooking spray.
2. Mix all the nuts and seeds, reserving ½ cup of the mixture.
Melt the chocolate in a metal dish over a pan of boiling water until smooth.
3. Toss in the nuts and fruits (except ½ cup, which will be reserved). To blend, mix fast.
4. Spoon chocolate-covered nut clusters onto the prepared baking sheet. Sprinkle with salt and a couple of the saved nuts and berries.

10 Mins

10 Mins

3

Maple Rosemary Nuts

 INGREDIENTS

- 2 tablespoons of unsalted butter, melted
- 3 tablespoons of maple syrup
- ½ teaspoon cayenne pepper
- 1 ½ tablespoon of fresh rosemary, finely chopped, divided
- 4 cups nut of your choice (e.g., pine nuts, pecans, walnuts, almonds)
- Sea salt, for sprinkling

 directions :

1. Preheat the oven to 350° F. Butter a large baking sheet that has been lined with foil.
2. Mix the melted butter, maple syrup, cayenne pepper, and 1 tablespoon rosemary in a mixing dish.
3. Toss in the nuts to coat them. Place the nuts on the baking sheet that has been prepared.
4. Preheat oven to 350°F and bake for 10 minutes. Stir again and bake for another 10 minutes, keeping an eye on them to ensure they don't burn.
5. Add the remaining rosemary and salt to the nuts.
6. Allow for complete cooling before storing in an airtight container.

10 Mins

40 Mins

3

Chapter 8

CONDIMENTS, SPREADS, AND DIPS

INGREDIENTS

- 1 cup of balsamic vinegar
- 1 cup of Cabernet Sauvignon
- 2 tablespoons of honey
- 1 tablespoon of unsalted butter, at room temperature

5 Mins

20 Mins

1

CABERNET BALSAMIC REDUCTION

 directions :

1. In a medium saucepan, mix the vinegar, wine, and honey. Over medium heat, stir, and bring to a simmer.
2. Cook for another 15 minutes, stirring regularly, to reduce the sauce. It should thicken and stay together like molasses.
3. Stir in the butter until it is entirely combined and emulsified after it has reduced by about half, then remove the pan from the heat.
4. Set aside to cool, then refrigerate for about 3 months in an airtight glass jar.

5 Mins **15 Mins** **3**

 INGREDIENTS

- 2 cups of extra-virgin olive oil
- 1 (10-ounce) jar artichoke hearts packed in oil, drained and roughly chopped
- 4 garlic cloves, thinly sliced
- 1 fresh or dried red chile
- Pinch of crushed red pepper
- Pinch of sea salt

ARTICHOKE-GARLIC CHILI OIL

 directions :

1. Mix all the ingredients in a medium pot.
2. Cook over medium heat until the oil is just ready to boil, about 15 minutes.
3. Remove the pot from the heat and set it aside to cool to room temperature.
4. Refrigerate for up to 2 months or store in a glass bottle at room temperature for up to 1 week.

- 1 shallot
- 2 garlic cloves, peeled
- 1 serrano pepper
- ¼ cup of red wine vinegar
- 2 bunches of fresh cilantro, leaves and tender stems finely chopped
- 1 bunch fresh parsley, leaves and tender stems finely chopped
- ¾ cup of extra-virgin olive oil
- 1½ teaspoons of sea salt
- Freshly ground black pepper

 15 Mins    0 Mins    3

CHIMICHURRI

 directions :

1. Combine the shallot, garlic, and serrano pepper in a food processor and process until smooth. Fill a small glass dish halfway with red wine vinegar and set aside for 5 minutes.
2. In a large glass dish, mix the cilantro and parsley.
3. Combine the cilantro and parsley with the shallot mixture. Season with sea salt and black pepper after adding the olive oil.
4. Combine all ingredients in a mixing bowl, cover, and chill for at least 3 hours before serving. Leftovers can be kept in the refrigerator for up to a week.

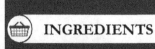

INGREDIENTS

- ¼ cup of honey
- ½ cup of champagne vinegar
- Pinch of sea salt
- 1½ teaspoons of whole-grain mustard
- Freshly ground black pepper

3 Mins

18 Mins

1

MUSTARD GASTRIQUE

 directions :

1. In a small nonstick pan or skillet, heat the honey over medium-low heat for approximately 5 minutes, or until it gets a rich amber color.
2. Pour in the vinegar and season with salt. Cook for another 3 minutes, stirring constantly with a wooden spoon to emulsify the mixture. Reduce the sauce to the consistency of thin maple syrup by turning the heat to low for about 10 minutes.
3. Remove the pan from the heat and add the whole-grain mustard and pepper. Warm the dish before serving.
4. Refrigerate the gastrique for up to two weeks in an airtight container. Before serving, slightly reheat the dish.

- 1 lemon
- 4 cups of whole raw almonds
- ¼ cup of extra-virgin olive oil
- 5 garlic cloves, peeled and lightly smashed
- 6 thyme sprigs
- 1 tablespoon of sea salt
- 1 teaspoon of freshly ground black pepper

 5 Mins 10 Mins  4

PAN-ROASTED GARLIC ALMONDS

 directions :

1. Remove all the yellow peel from the lemon with a vegetable peeler and set it aside.
2. Mix the almonds and olive oil in a large skillet. Cook for 2 to 3 minutes over medium heat, stirring to coat.
3. Combine the garlic, thyme, and lemon peel in a mixing bowl. Season to taste with salt and pepper.
4. Cook, stirring occasionally so that the nuts don't burn, for 5 to 8 minutes, or until they have a fragrant, nutty scent and are crispy.
5. Allow it cool for about 5 minutes before eating. Alternatively, keep at room temperature for up to a week in an airtight container.

INGREDIENTS

- 20 Medjool dates (or any variety), pitted
- 1 teaspoon of vanilla bean paste
- ½ teaspoon of sea salt
- ½ cup of unsweetened almond milk

10 Mins

0 Mins

2

DATE CARAMEL

directions :

1. Combine all the ingredients in a high-powered blender. Blend until completely smooth; this might take a minute, so be patient and stir as needed. If necessary, add a nut milk to get the smooth texture.
2. Refrigerate for up to 3 days in an airtight container, although it's best served fresh.

 INGREDIENTS

- 8 cups of whole milk
- 2 cups of heavy whipping cream
- 1½ teaspoons of sea salt
- 6 tablespoons of distilled white vinegar

 15 Mins

 15 Mins

 4

FRESH RICOTTA

 directions :

1. Place a fine-mesh sieve over a big bowl and line it with cheesecloth.
2. Mix the milk, cream, and salt in a large stockpot. Bring to a boil over high heat, then reduce to low heat.
3. Pour the vinegar into the milk mixture and stir. Remove the pot from the heat and set it aside for 5 minutes. The whey and curds will separate.
4. Pour the mixture into a sieve lined with cheesecloth and set aside to drain.
5. Serve immediately or keep refrigerated for up to 1 week in an airtight container.

- 2 (16-ounce) cans chickpeas, rinse and drained
- 1 cup of tahini
- ½ cup of extra-virgin olive oil, plus more for drizzling
- 1½ teaspoons of fresh lemon juice
- 1 garlic clove, chopped
- 1 teaspoon of sea salt
- 8 ounces of goat cheese, divided
- Moroccan spice blend (optional)

10 Mins

0 Mins

5

GOAT CHEESE HUMMUS

 directions :

1. Combine the chickpeas, tahini, olive oil, lemon juice, garlic, and sea salt in a food processor. Blend until the mixture is completely smooth.
2. Blend in half of the goat cheese until it is completely smooth. Scoop everything into a medium bowl with a silicone spatula.
3. Crumble the leftover goat cheese and add it to the hummus mixture with the spatula.
4. Drizzle with olive oil and, if preferred, a pinch of Moroccan spice blend before serving. Refrigerate for up to one month in an airtight container.

 INGREDIENTS

- 1 pound of pancetta, cubed
- 1 medium yellow onion, diced
- 4 shallots, diced
- 3 garlic cloves, minced
- ½ cup of packed brown sugar
- ½ cup of pure maple syrup
- 2 tablespoons of balsamic vinegar
- 2 tablespoons of apple cider vinegar

10 Mins

30 Mins

1

PANCETTA-ONION JAM

 directions :

1. Brown the pancetta in a large skillet or Dutch oven over high heat until crispy, about 8 to 10 minutes. Transfer to a small bowl with a slotted spoon. The rendered pancetta fat should be left in the pan.
2. Add the onion and shallots to the pan and cook over medium-high heat for approximately 10 minutes, or until they caramelize and turn amber-brown.
3. Stir in the garlic for 2 to 3 minutes, until aromatic. Combine the brown sugar, maple syrup, and both tablespoons of vinegar in a mixing bowl. 5 minutes of constant stirring
4. Return the pancetta and any remaining fat to the pan. Cook for about 5 minutes, or until the flavors have blended and the mixture has thickened into a thick jam.
5. Allow it to cool completely before serving.

INGREDIENTS

- 3 cups of Greek yogurt
- 1 small shallot, minced
- 1 garlic clove, minced
- ¼ cup of finely chopped fresh parsley
- ¼ cup of finely chopped fresh basil
- ¼ cup of finely chopped fresh chives
- 1 tablespoon of finely chopped fresh dill
- 2 tablespoons of extra-virgin olive oil
- 2 tablespoons of champagne vinegar (or white wine vinegar)
- 1 small cucumber, peeled, seeded, and minced
- 2 teaspoons of sea salt
- Freshly ground black pepper

15 Mins **0 Mins** **4**

CREAMY HERB YOGURT SAUCE

directions :

1. In a large mixing bowl, whisk together the Greek yogurt, shallot, garlic, and chopped herbs.
2. Combine the olive oil and vinegar in a mixing bowl. Mix vigorously until everything is completely blended.
3. Add the cucumber and season to taste with sea salt and freshly ground pepper. If necessary, taste and season again.
4. Refrigerate for 30 minutes before serving. Keep refrigerated for up to a week in an airtight container.

Chapter 9

PICKLES, BITES, AND BREADS

BRINED CUCUMBER RIBBONS

 **INGREDIENTS**

- 1 cup of warm water
- ⅓ cup of distilled white vinegar
- 2 teaspoons of sugar
- 1 teaspoon of sea salt
- ½ teaspoon of ground white pepper
- 4 English cucumbers

Method

1. Mix the warm water, vinegar, sugar, salt, and white pepper in a large measuring cup.
2. Peel the cucumbers all the way down to the seeds using a vegetable peeler, forming long strands of cucumber ribbons.
3. Separate the ribbons into two pint-sized jars.
4. Pour the vinegar mixture over the ribbons and screw on the lids, ensuring that they are completely immersed.
5. Allow to brine for 25 minutes at room temperature before serving, or refrigerate for up to 1 week.

10Mins

0 Mins

1

OVEN-DRIED STRAWBERRIES

 INGREDIENTS

- 1 pound of fresh strawberries, sliced
- 2 tablespoons of raw sugar
- Nonstick cooking spray

Method

1. Mix the cut berries with the raw sugar in a large mixing dish to coat. Allow for a 25-minute rest period.
2. Preheat the oven to 200 ℉.
3. Spray a rimmed baking sheet with nonstick cooking spray and line it with parchment paper.
4. Strain the strawberries, but keep the liquid to make a syrup. On the prepared baking sheet, arrange the strawberries in a single layer.
5. Bake for 30 minutes, flip the baking sheet, and bake for another 30 minutes. Bake for another 30 minutes, turning the baking sheet halfway through. After 1½ hours, turn the strawberries over and continue the drying process, turning the baking sheet every 30 minutes.
6. Bake for up to 3 hours, until they have darkened in color and are dry around the edges.

25Mins

3 hrs

2

ROSEMARY-LEMON CASTELVETRANO OLIVES

 INGREDIENTS

- 1 (20-ounce) jar Castelvetrano olives, drained
- ½ cup of extra-virgin olive oil
- 5 garlic cloves, thinly sliced
- 4 rosemary sprigs, cut in half
- 1 lemon

Method

1. Toss the olives with the olive oil in a large mixing dish.
2. Add the rosemary sprigs and garlic slices.
3. Peel large pieces of lemon peel into the bowl with a vegetable peeler. Split the lemon and squeeze the juice into the mixing basin.
4. Mix everything together, cover, and set aside for at least 1 hour before serving at room temperature.
5. Keep refrigerated for up to a week in an airtight container.

10Mins

0 Mins

4

APRICOT-CHIPOTLE GUMMIES

INGREDIENTS

- 2 cups of apricot nectar
- ¼ cup of grass-fed gelatin (or 4 packets plain gelatin)
- 1 teaspoon of chipotle puree (from canned chipotle peppers in adobo sauce)
- ¼ cup of honey

Method

1. In a medium saucepan, pour the apricot nectar. Sprinkle the gelatin over the nectar, mix, and set aside for 5 minutes to allow the gelatin to bloom.
2. Increase the heat to medium-high and whisk for 2 to 3 minutes, or until the gelatin has completely dissolved.
3. Stir in the chipotle puree until everything is fully combined.
4. Stir in the honey and heat, stirring constantly, for approximately 5 minutes, or until the mixture boils.
5. Stir everything together to ensure it's all dissolved and blended nicely. Remove the pan from the heat and pour the mixture into an 8-inch square silicone mold or a glass baking pan.
6. Chill for at least 3 hours or until firm. Cut into 1-inch squares if you aren't using a mold. Refrigerate for up to 2 weeks if stored in an airtight container.

5 Mins

15 Mins

1

ROASTED VINE CAMPARI TOMATOES

 INGREDIENTS

- 2 pounds on-the-vine Campari tomatoes
- 2 tablespoons of extra-virgin olive oil
- Sea salt
- Freshly ground black pepper

Method

1. Preheat the oven to 350 ℉. Using parchment paper, line a rimmed baking sheet.
2. Arrange the tomatoes in a single layer on the prepared baking sheet, ensuring that the vines are intact.
3. Pour a considerable amount of olive oil and salt over the tomatoes. Season them with black pepper.
4. Roast for 15 minutes or until the skins split. Warm the dish before serving.

3 Mins

15 Mins

8

PICKLED RED ONION AND FENNEL

 INGREDIENTS

- ⅔ cup of water
- ½ cup of apple cider vinegar
- 1 tablespoon of honey
- 1 teaspoon of sea salt
- 1 red onion, halved and sliced into paper-thin slices
- 1 fennel bulb, fronds trimmed, bulb halved and thinly sliced

Method

1. Mix the water, apple cider vinegar, honey, and salt in a small saucepan and heat over medium heat, stirring constantly, until the mixture is simmering, then remove from the heat.

2. Fill a quart-size jar halfway with onion and fennel slices. Make sure the onion and fennel are well immersed in the heated vinegar mixture. Allow it to cool before reinstalling the cover.

3. Refrigerate for at least 25 minutes or up to 1 week before serving.

15 Mins

0 Mins

1

DUCK CONFIT

 INGREDIENTS

- 2 bone-in, skin-on whole duck legs (thigh plus drumstick)
- 2 tablespoons of duck fat
- Sea salt

Method

1. Preheat the oven to 350 ℉.
2. In a small baking pan, combine the duck legs and duck fat.
3. Roast in the oven for about 2 hours, or until the meat is extremely tender.
4. Transfer the legs to a chopping board and use 2 forks to shred the meat and skin away from the bones.
5. Combine the skin and meat with any remaining rendered fat in the pan. Season with a pinch of salt.
6. Refrigerate the confit in its fat for up to 3 months in an airtight container.

3 Mins

2 Hrs

4

MINI CHAFFLES

🧺 INGREDIENTS

- 1 cup of shredded mozzarella (preferably freshly shredded)
- 2 large eggs, beaten
- 2 tablespoons of almond flour
- Nonstick cooking spray

Method

1. Preheat medium-high small waffle iron.
2. Mix the shredded mozzarella, eggs, and almond flour in a small mixing dish. Stir until all of the ingredients are properly blended.
3. Divide the mixture into four parts that are equal in size. Spray the prepared waffle iron with cooking spray, scoop one part onto the waffle iron, close the top, and cook until crispy. This should only take 1 to 2 minutes, but be sure to read the directions on your waffle iron. Carry on with the remaining pieces in the same manner.
4. Remove from the heat and set aside to cool for 2 to 3 minutes before serving.

5 Mins

6 Mins

4

THYME SHORTBREAD

 INGREDIENTS

- 1 vanilla bean
- 3 sticks unsalted butter, softened
- 1 cup of sugar
- 3½ cups of all-purpose flour
- ¼ teaspoon of sea salt
- Grated zest of 1 lemon
- Leaves from 8 thyme sprigs

Method

1. Cut the vanilla bean lengthwise with the point of a paring knife. Remove the seeds with a scraper and set them aside.
2. Mix the butter and sugar in the bowl of an electric stand mixer fitted with the paddle attachment or in a large mixing basin with a handheld electric mixer. Add the vanilla bean seeds and whip them into the butter mixture until it's all mixed.
3. Reduce the speed of the mixer to low and add the flour, salt, and lemon zest, mixing until thoroughly blended. Mix in the thyme leaves until the dough is completely mixed.
4. Place the dough on a large piece of plastic wrap and roll it up. Fold the wrap over the dough and roll it into a log approximately 2 inches in diameter using your hands. Refrigerate for 15 to 20 minutes or until firm.
5. Preheat the oven to 350°F. Line a rimmed baking sheet with parchment paper.
6. Slice the dough into ¼-inch thick rounds, and arrange them on the prepared baking sheet. Bake until the edges are golden, 20 to 25 minutes. Transfer to a cooling rack to cool.
7. Store in an airtight container at room temperature for up to 1 week.

15 Mins

25 Mins

24

YORKSHIRE PUDDING

 INGREDIENTS

- 6 teaspoons of avocado oil (or light olive oil)
- 2 large eggs
- ⅔ cup of all-purpose flour
- ½ cup of whole milk
- Pinch of sea salt

Method

1. Preheat the oven to 425 ℉.
2. In a regular muffin tray, sprinkle ½ tsp of oil into each compartment. Place the pan the oven and heat for 10 minutes.
3. In a blender, add the eggs, flour, milk, and salt and process for 15 to 20 seconds, or until smooth.
4. Carefully take the muffin pan from the oven, using oven mitts since the oil will be quite hot. Return the pans to the oven and pour the batter equally into each section.
5. Bake for 12 to 15 minutes, or until the Yorkshire puddings are puffy and golden brown. Warm the dish before serving.

10Mins

15 Mins

12

Chapter 10

Anytime Boards

Hungry Man Stew

 INGREDIENTS

- 1 pound of ground beef
- 1 medium onion, sliced
- 1 tablespoon of cooking oil
- 2 cups of carrots, diced
- 3 russet potatoes, diced
- 1 16-ounce can kidney beans, drained
- ¼ cup of uncooked long grain rice
- 1 8-ounce can tomato sauce
- 4 cups of water
- ¼ teaspoon of chili powder
- ¼ cup of Worcestershire sauce
- Non-stick cooking spray

 directions :

1. Spray nonstick cooking spray on the slow cooker.
2. Heat the oil in a skillet and fry the meat and onion. Drain the fat from the meat and place it in a slow cooker.
3. Combine the carrots, potatoes, kidney beans, rice, tomato sauce, water, chili powder, and Worcestershire sauce in a large mixing bowl.
4. Cover and cook on LOW for 6-8 hours. Continue cooking for another hour if the potatoes and rice are still too firm after 6 hours, then check for doneness every 30 minutes or so.

10 Mins

60 Mins

4

Pioneer Goulash

INGREDIENTS

- 1 pound of ground beef
- 1 cup of yellow onion, diced
- ½ cup of celery, chopped
- 1 tablespoon of jarred minced garlic
- 1 15-ounce can diced tomatoes
- 1 15-ounce can tomato sauce
- 1 15-ounce can kidney beans, drained
- 1½ cups of water or tomato-based vegetable juice
- 1 tablespoon of Worcestershire sauce
- 1 tablespoon of soy sauce
- 1 teaspoon of oregano
- 1 teaspoon of thyme
- 1 teaspoon of paprika
- 1 teaspoon of salt
- 1 teaspoon of pepper
- 1-2 cups of uncooked elbow macaroni

directions :

1. Preheat the coals in the Dutch oven and place the oven on top of them.
2. Add the ground beef, onion, celery, and garlic to the oven after it has heated up. Cook until the beef is browned, about 10 minutes.
3. Combine the tomatoes, tomato sauce, kidney beans, vegetable juice, Worcestershire sauce, and soy sauce in a large mixing bowl. Continue to cook until the liquid is hot and bubbling.
4. Add oregano, thyme, paprika, salt, and pepper to taste. Continue to cook for another 5 minutes. Cover and continue cooking for another 30 minutes, or until the elbow macaroni is soft.

10 Mins

30 Mins

5

Beef Chili

INGREDIENTS

- 1 ¼ pounds of lean ground beef
- 3 tablespoons of grass-fed ghee
- 1 carrot, chopped
- 2 celery stalks, finely chopped
- 4 tomatoes, chopped
- ½ teaspoon of cumin seeds, ground
- 1 teaspoon of oregano
- ½ teaspoon of cinnamon
- 1 teaspoon of sea salt
- 3 cups of Bok choy, chopped
- 1 avocado, pitted and peeled

directions :

1. In a soup pot, heat 3 tbsp grass-fed ghee over medium heat, then brown the meat.
2. Cook for 30 minutes with the carrots, celery, tomatoes, cumin, oregano, cinnamon, and salt.
3. Stir in the Bok choy and avocado and simmer for another 10 minutes, or until the Bok choy has wilted and the avocado is warm.

10 Mins

30 Mins

4

Classic Beef Chili

 INGREDIENTS

- 3 tablespoons of butter
- 1 pound of lean ground beef
- Salt and pepper to taste
- 1 teaspoon of Dijon mustard
- 1 spring onion, finely chopped
- 1 clove garlic, minced
- 1 teaspoon of paprika
- 1 teaspoon of dried oregano
- 1 red chili, diced
- 1 (16-ounce) can of red kidney beans
- 2 cups of tomato sauce
- 1 cup of beef stock
- 2 tablespoons of freshly chopped basil
- 2 tablespoons of freshly chopped parsley

directions :

1. Boil the beef stock, then add the ground beef.
2. Add salt, pepper, Dijon mustard, spring onion, garlic, oregano, paprika, and chili to taste.
3. After 5 minutes, add the beans, tomato sauce, and beef stock and cook for another 5 minutes.
4. Allow for 20 minutes of cooking time. Sprinkle with parsley and basil and cook for 10 more minutes.

10 Mins

30 Mins

4

Beef Cheesy Chili

 INGREDIENTS

- 3 tablespoons of olive oil
- 1 pound of lean ground beef
- Salt and pepper to taste
- 1 teaspoon of tomato paste
- 1 teaspoon of onion powder
- 1 clove garlic, minced
- 1 teaspoon of paprika
- 1 teaspoon of dried oregano
- 1 red chili, diced
- 1 (16-ounce) can sweet corn
- 2 cups of tomato sauce
- 1 cup of beef stock
- 2 tablespoons of freshly chopped parsley
- 1 cup of grated cheddar cheese

directions :

1. Heat olive oil in a pan.
2. Add the ground beef to the pan.
3. Add salt, pepper, tomato paste, onion powder, garlic, oregano, paprika, and chili to taste.
4. Stir in the corn, tomato sauce, and beef stock after 5 minutes of cooking. Cook for 20 minutes more.
5. Add the parsley and simmer for another 10 minutes.
6. Sprinkle the grated cheddar cheese over the top just before serving.

10 Mins

50 Mins

4

Slow Cooker Simple Cheesy Chili Recipe

 INGREDIENTS

- 1 pound of ground beef, browned, drained
- 2 packets chili seasoning
- 2 cans (14½ ounces each) tomatoes with chipotle chilies, diced
- ¾ pound of elbow macaroni
- Cheese, grated and sour cream (optional)

directions :

1. In your slow cooker, combine the first three ingredients.
2. Cook for 8 hours on low heat.
3. Cook the pasta and add it to the crockpot when the steak is almost done. Allow for another half-hour of cooking time.
4. To serve, transfer everything to a dish or plate and top with the optional additions (if wanted).

10 Mins

50 Mins

4

Garlic and Spice Beef Chili

INGREDIENTS

- 1 pound of lean beef, browned
- 1 cup of onion, diced
- 6 cloves garlic, crushed and minced
- 2 jalapeño peppers, sliced
- ½ cup of tomato paste
- 2 cups of stewed tomatoes, with liquid
- ¼ cup of canned green chilies
- 1 cup of tomato juice
- ¼ cup of chili powder
- 1 tablespoon of ground cumin
- 2 teaspoons of cocoa powder
- 1 teaspoon of mustard powder
- 1 teaspoon of onion powder
- 1 teaspoon of salt
- 1 teaspoon of black pepper
- 1 teaspoon of oregano
- ½ cup of sour cream
- 1 avocado, sliced
- ¼ cup of fresh cilantro

directions :

1. Combine the onion, garlic, jalapeño peppers, tomato paste, stewed tomatoes, green chilies, and tomato juice on top of the ground beef. Mix thoroughly.
2. Add chili powder, cumin, cocoa powder, mustard, onion powder, salt, black pepper, and oregano to the chili. Remix the ingredients.
3. Toss the chili with sour cream, avocado, and fresh cilantro before serving.

10 Mins

30 Mins

4

Chili Con Carne I

 INGREDIENTS

- 1 10½ ounce can hot-style vegetable juice
- 1 15½ ounce can diced tomatoes
- 3 green chilies, undrained
- 1 pound of ground beef
- 1 large onion, diced
- 15½ ounces water

directions :

1. Preheat a skillet with cooking spray on the stove. Cook the onions until the meat is brown and tender.
2. Add the ground beef and heat until the meat is well cooked.
3. In a slow cooker, add the ground beef mixture, undrained tomatoes, beans, green chilies, and vegetable juice.
4. Using the chopped tomato can, add a full can of water. Cover and stir.
Cook for 6-7 hours on low heat.

10 Mins

50 Mins

4

Noodles with Butter

INGREDIENTS

- 16 ounces of fettuccine noodles
- 6 tablespoons of butter
- 1/3 cup of grated parmesan cheese
- A pinch of salt
- A pinch of pepper
- 4 cups of water

directions :

1. Fill a large pot with water and add in the salt.
2. Add the fettuccini noodles to the pot and boil them.
3. Once the water has boiled, drain it and set it aside.
4. Place the noodles in a saucepan that has been left empty.
5. Add the butter, salt, and pepper, as well as the grated parmesan cheese.
Combine all ingredients and serve!

10 Mins

40 Mins

5

Conclusion

In certain areas, charcuterie also involves the preservation of fish using similar techniques to make delicacies such as smoked salmon, lox, and pickled herring.

Nowadays, the word "charcuterie" refers to the serving of preserved meats or seafood with cheeses, fruits, and a variety of other accompaniments during parties and celebrations. Charcuterie spreads serve as a focal point for family and friends to mingle while enjoying an array of flavors and textures from across the world at get-togethers.

Charcuterie boards are not only attractive, but they also include a variety of flavors and nibbles for a no-fuss party snack.

It's simple to put together a cheese and sausage board that everyone will like. Adding basic tastes from commonplace products requires very little prep time and only a minute to put together.

Made in the USA
Coppell, TX
07 December 2022

88072946R00077